Women M
a Differe

D0345782

Marigold Best taught Spanish for many years before becoming Latin America Programme Coordinator for Quaker Peace & Service. She managed small projects in the region and by speaking and writing kept British Friends informed about Latin American issues. Now retired, she helps to strengthen links with Latin American Quakers and takes British Friends to visit Cuban Friends. She greatly values her cooperation with Pamela Hussey and hopes to continue working in an ecumenical context.

Pamela Hussey has been with the Latin America section of the Catholic Institute for International Relations since 1981. She visited Central America, especially El Salvador, six times between 1982 and 1994, and has produced two books, *Free from Fear: Women in El Salvador's Church*, published by CIIR in 1989, and, with Marigold Best, *Life Out of Death: The feminine spirit in El Salvador*, published by CIIR in 1996. She was awarded the MBE in the Queen's Birthday Honours List in 2000, for 'services to human rights in Latin America'. She is a member of the Roman Catholic religious congregation Society of the Holy Child Jesus.

Women Making a Difference

MARIGOLD BEST
AND
PAMELA HUSSEY

First published in Great Britain in 2001 by
SPCK, Holy Trinity Church,
Marylebone Road, London NW1 4DU
and
Catholic Institute for International Relations,
Unit 3, Canonbury Yard, 190a New North Road,
London N1 7BY

The editors and publishers gratefully acknowledge permission
to reproduce the following material:
'A Prayer for Abundant Life', Keri Wehlander, in *Wisdom is
Calling*, G. Duncan, ed., Canterbury Press, 1999.

British Library Cataloguing-in-Publication Data

A catalogue record for this book is available from
the British Library

ISBN 0-281-05294-8

Typeset by Mark Heslington, Scarborough, North Yorkshire
Printed in Great Britain by Omnia Books, Glasgow

Contents

Foreword

When I was approached to write this foreword, the authors were kind enough to say they were asking me 'because you are a woman making a difference'. My immediate reaction was to think, 'What *do* they mean, I'm not making a difference to anything.' I suspect that's a typical woman's reaction, and I wonder why? It's as if, somewhere along the line, we subconsciously pick up the idea that whatever success is, it doesn't include what we happen to be doing. And if I catch myself thinking this, with the good fortune I have had, of an inspiring education, a secure home and an interesting job, how much more likely is this to be the mental attitude of many of the women whose voices we hear in this book, who are having to fight all the way for education, job opportunities and the renewal of their community life. But if it is, they haven't let it stop them.

This is an inspiring book to read: how could it not be? Marigold and Pamela have found women up and down England who are making a difference at every level of our national life: in radical engagement with their local communities, in reinvigorating traditional women's organizations, in entering into dialogue with some of the 'big beasts' of the corporate world.

On one level the book works as a do-it-yourself tutorial in direct action: how to facilitate groups, empower people to take responsibility for their situation, set up non-hierarchical structures, raise funds from unpromising sources, engage power structures with very different points of view. On another level our politicians could garner very practical recommendations for making effective use of government funding: the crucial importance of retaining further and continuing education to provide training, especially for women, comes through in many of these stories.

One piece of advice, offered in an economic context, rang particularly true to me from my very different personal experience in the ecumenical setting, and that is the importance of hanging on to the reality of one's arguments. 'It has happened because we stuck to our viewpoint.' There is always a tendency in any dialogue to try to be reasonable, to accommodate the other person's position, to make use of the other's arguments to show that one is not a stranger in their world; and it may be that women are particularly susceptible to this kind of thinking. But it is worth learning that this can be to limit one's effectiveness: the kind of conversation most useful for progress is one which clearly identifies the distance yet to be travelled.

One may reasonably ask: why is this book only about women? Are women specifically cut out for this kind of work? The authors rightly eschew analysis, and let their contributors speak for themselves, but the combined voices of this book suggest one probable answer. Women often have other connections into society, through family responsibilities or through their community lives; they should perhaps be better able than men, who may be trapped in a single, working-life, dimension, to retain a sense of proportion about the structures they're taking on and have less excuse for allowing themselves to be consumed by them.

This is a book about engagement and detachment. I was conscious as I read it of the two meanings of the word 'care', which T. S. Eliot beautifully captures in his poem, 'Ash Wednesday': 'Teach us to care and not to care; teach us to sit still'. These women are not, of course, sitting still. All these lives stand as testimonies to women's determination to care, to do something about the situation in which they find themselves, to lessen its inequalities, lift its poverty, empower themselves and their neighbours for change. But the book is also shot through with reminders of the need *not* to care, in the sense of caring about what people might think, or worrying about the obstacles laid in the way. 'You just pay no attention.'

And just to encourage you, the book is not all earnest endeavour. There is elegance, if not exactly fragrance, there is fashion, and there is humour. Look out for Sarah as she begins the long wait for future generations to grasp the real test which God had set for Abraham: 'as if I hadn't got enough to do'.

Rowena Loverance
Co-President, Churches Together in England

Introduction

In early 1996 our book *Life out of Death: The Feminine Spirit in El Salvador* was published by the Catholic Institute for International Relations. It was based on conversations we had had with a wide variety of women in El Salvador who shared with us the stories of their activities and experiences before, during and since the terrible years of civil war from 1980 to 1992. Their indomitable spirit and determination to keep on striving to build a better society, and to develop their own role within it, had been deeply moving, and producing the book had been such a learning experience for us, that we wanted to follow it up in some way. After much discussion it struck us that we, and probably the general public, really knew very little about what women in our own country are doing to change things for the better and to transcend their traditional roles, and that it would be interesting to find out. Our quest over nearly two years (May 1998–February 2000) has resulted in this book, which aims to make visible those women whose lives make a difference, but who are not for the most part officially recognized.

We do not claim to offer a complete picture of women's activities throughout the United Kingdom – that would take several lifetimes. One of the many values of this book (we are blowing not our own trumpets but those of the women whose stories we tell!) is to demonstrate that, wherever you happen to be based, if you ask around and follow up leads you will find women doing marvellous things to make things better for themselves and others in all sorts of ways.

People often ask us, 'Where on earth did you start?' Not unnaturally, since Pamela is a Roman Catholic religious sister and Marigold a Quaker (both of us ecumenically minded), we had contacts within the Churches who put us in touch with a wide range of people and projects. So we are pleased to reflect activities

1

not only of Catholics and Quakers, but also of Anglicans, Baptists, ELIM Pentecostal and Methodists. But while we are glad to show that Christianity, in spite of the disparaging press it often gets, is in fact motivating creative and inspiring initiatives all over the place, we also show that people of other faiths, and people with no religious affiliation at all, are equally motivated to love their neighbours. The particular form of words, 'Love your neighbour as yourself' may be identified with Christianity, but other faiths express similar sentiments, and the spirit behind the words is present everywhere.

'Love was the first motion,' wrote American Quaker John Woolman in 1763, sitting in his tent in a rainstorm, on his way, humbly and respectfully, to get to know the 'Red Indians' as fellow human beings. They got on very well. And love in that sense of reaching out to others as fellow human beings is the common denominator in all the stories in this book. The beautiful and hopeful thing is that such reaching out reproduces itself. We met women who, like too many women in this country, had not been treated as fully human and had come to think of themselves as worthless, but who, by being welcomed and valued, blossomed into their full potential and are now reaching out to other women. Over and over again we saw how welcoming and valuing is the essential 'first motion' which can enable disempowered people to move forward and perhaps take advantage of resources like counselling, education and training. It is likewise what enables those who reach out also to receive. As the volunteers in the drop-in centre in Salford told us, 'They give us much more than we give them.' And it is the attitude which our friends working at the international level are trying to encourage in multinational businesses and institutions like the World Bank!

The geographical spread of the places we have visited has not been enormous, but it has been quite diverse: London, Oxford, Birmingham, Loughborough, York, Sheffield, Salford and the Newcastle area. We could have gone on following up leads which would have taken us to Wales, Scotland and Northern Ireland, as well as to many other places in England, but we already had so much marvellous material that we thought we would go ahead and produce a 'starter pack', hoping that other people would follow our example of trying to make visible what is too often invisible – women's invaluable contribution to making our society more fully human.

Deciding how to organize all this material has been difficult. We started with no preconceived plan, but as we followed our noses we realized what a wide range of ground we were covering, and occasionally tried to fill in what seemed important gaps. For instance, we realized that what little we knew about some of the household names among women's organizations might be at least out of date, if not plain wrong. And so it proved when we met with the Young Women's Christian Association (Christian-based) and the Women's Institute (constitutionally secular). Sometimes jewels were dropped in our lap by pure serendipity – for instance, a passing reference at a conference to a woman who had single-handedly begun to change the lives of women on a grim housing estate led us to Catherine Moore.

All the stories are jewels in their different ways and we have tried to string them together in some kind of logical order, starting with individual initiatives and going through to initiatives at international level. The thread uniting them all is the fact of women making a difference, working to effect positive changes in society, or trying to maintain hope and humanity in the face of destructive changes.

We are deeply grateful to the many people who have given us leads, arranged meetings for us, or given us accommodation: Bernadette Askins, Pat Daly, Jo Forster, Mary Jefferson, Kathleen King, Jean Mayland, Catriona McPhail, Frances Morgan, Stephen Petter, James Ramsay, Chris Rowland, Nan Saeki, Carol Saker, Jane Sherwin, Mike Simpson, Pat Sumpter, Alison Webster.

We want to thank from the bottom of our hearts all the women who so generously shared their reflections and experiences with two people who were after all total strangers to most of them. Meeting them was a deeply enriching experience for us, as we hope it will also be for our readers.

We also want to thank the Catholic Institute for International Relations and the Society of the Holy Child Jesus very warmly for all their support and encouragement.

❧ 1 ❧

A Heaven in the Midst of Hell

One of the users of the Lighthouse Project started by Catherine Moore in Halesowen, Birmingham, when asked what the Lighthouse meant in her life, answered without a moment's hesitation, 'A heaven in the midst of hell.'

The Lighthouse Project is located behind an inconspicuous door marked 'Community Flat', on the edge of a run-down housing estate. Once inside the door, which was unlocked, all was bright and welcoming. Catherine arrived and told us how she came to be doing this work.

ONE WOMAN'S VISION

'Well, it really did take me completely by surprise! I've only been a Christian for seven years – before that I'd been to Sunday School as a child, and that was it. But I became a single parent of twins – my husband left me when they were five weeks old. So that was quite traumatic. Someone introduced me to the Lord then and it was very much a turning point in my life. I subsequently, as a Christian, felt that I needed to forgive my husband for what he had done, and we were reconciled. I got pregnant again, and had another child, and he did the same thing to me again, and left when my little girl was ten weeks old. So I've been on my own quite a lot!

'I've been a florist for 25 years. I absolutely love my work and I thought that I would do that for ever. But as I got to know God and wanted to walk his path, there came the day when I said, "Well Lord, I want to give you all of me, and I want to do whatever you would have me do", and that was it, really. I prayed that prayer and God responded and put me in a place where I became aware of the needs of women, particularly single parents, but also young

4

women who may be married but on very low incomes, or on benefits, both partners out of work, living in poverty really. Young teenagers that have been forced out of their homes, and have all come to live on this estate. I became aware of this because my children started school, and I was talking to mums in the playground, and I was quite staggered at how lonely people were, that on the surface seem very OK, but are desperately lonely, feeling completely isolated. A lot of people suffering from depression and just not able to cope with the simplest dilemma, because they've got no one to talk to. The family unit's all broken down, your mother lives miles away.

Nowhere to go

'And here particularly, because this estate is the way it is, with vandalism and drug abuse and prostitution (you wouldn't believe it, looking at it, but that's how it is), people become very insular and they're in their homes and they stay in their homes. There's no communal place for people to come together and share, so I found that a lot of ladies were wandering round the town and not wanting to go home, and probably spending money that they couldn't afford, in the tea and coffee shops all day. And I thought this is so sad, it's such a waste of lives. I had no idea what people had gone through to get to where they were, but I had a sense of the struggle that people were experiencing. It was just that God laid it on my heart and I was suddenly very burdened by it.

It's just a dream

'I'd never been in community work at all, I just thought it might be a nice idea to open somewhere where people could go and have coffee, and instead of just standing in the playground sharing difficulties with each other, they could at least be under cover and having a coffee and perhaps be able to make friends with each other. The problems aren't that big, often, and if we can share them they can be solved. But if they aren't solved, and another problem comes along, and that's compounded with another problem, before you know where you are somebody's been referred to the mental health clinic, because they're clinically depressed. It's as simple as that, sadly that's the truth of it.

'So it was a question of where do we have this? I'm a member of the local church, the Zion Christian Centre, which is a huge building, but I just knew that people wouldn't want to go to a church. They would be too intimidated or wonder what we were doing, whether we were trying to convert them, increase the numbers or whatever. So a friend of mine and I prayer-walked the town, unsuccessfully, for a day – you can cover quite a lot of ground in a day – and we didn't find anything. That evening I had a dream that the council had given us premises on this estate, and we were open and there were various women in, and there was the smell of coffee and there was the smell of toast and a lovely buzz of conversation, and people were getting to know each other, it was a wonderful atmosphere. I woke up and I thought, "Oh, wow, fantastic!" So I phoned my friend and said, "I've had this wonderful dream, but, you know, it's just a dream"; and she said, "Well, let's phone the council and see what they say".'

The dream comes true

'So we did and by 12 o'clock that day we'd been given these premises, which was a miracle, a miracle. We didn't know what they were, but we were told that they were premises that we could have if we wanted them. So we came to have a look, just thinking that there would be a little room, but of course there's more, a big meeting room and four other rooms so we can have an office and my mind absolutely went off – Gosh, we could do this, and we could do this, and we could actually provide counselling, and services like pregnancy-testing, because there are a lot of young people getting pregnant here. Lots of things, marriage guidance counselling and parenting classes – it lent itself to so much. So the idea suddenly developed and snowballed into a Family Centre. But we hadn't got a penny! We set about thinking – this is obviously a very good idea but it needs research, and if we're going to get support we need to have some professional bodies or organizations behind the concept to give it some sort of validity and professionalism. So one of my first contacts was with the church that I'm a member of. We needed to raise money so I asked if the church would adopt the idea, so we could use their charitable status in order to raise funds. It instantly gave the project some credibility.

Never a negative response

'Then I spent 12 months networking the community and never met with a negative response. It's absolutely incredible – because I've been in sales as well, and I know how difficult it is to get to speak to the appropriate person, and to get decisions from people, it's a very lengthy process. But I always managed to speak to the person in charge, I always managed to get an answer on the phone there and then. We put together a portfolio of support for the project and decided to open five days a week if we could find someone to run it.

Who will run it?

'I was sitting in church one day and praying and saying, "Lord, there must be somebody in this church" – we have a very large congregation of about 400–600, so I was sitting there saying there must be someone who was absolutely ideal to run this Centre – and in that moment I knew it was me, and I almost heard the Lord saying, "It's you!"; and I was saying, "No, no, it can't be right, I'm a florist! I can't do that." But I could almost hear this voice saying, "It's you, I've chosen you." I was happy to take up the challenge but that's when the complications started and the difficulty of explaining things to my family. It's hard as a single parent, to give up an income and step out in faith that God would provide for myself and the family, and also provide for the Centre, because we needed resources, we needed equipment. So as you can imagine, there was a tremendous amount of prayer for all these things, and for volunteers.

God has provided

'It's just been absolutely staggering how God has provided for the needs of the Centre. We estimated that we would need £10,000 to operate for a year, but we very quickly realized that we needed crèche facilities, and we needed staff for that, and the whole thing was growing very quickly, and we needed more funds. God provided £43,000 for us in the first year. I do most of the fundraising. I've never done any before – I literally just write a letter and send it off, and pray over it, and then when the money comes in, it's staggering.

'We're just coming up to the end of our second year and the Lord has provided £86,000 for us this year. I am just completely in awe about this. I write the letters but that's all I do, the project is so blessed, God's hand is on it, he just wants to reach out to these hurt and damaged people and give them a touch of his love through everybody that comes in and everybody that has given us something. Every single item of anything in the building has been given, we haven't had to buy anything at all, apart from the photocopier, but somebody donated the money for that. Everything else has just turned up. We run a toy library and all the toys go into little bags in pretty fabrics. One day we had to say a quick prayer for more fabrics because we hadn't got any money. And half an hour later the buzzer went from the door downstairs and when we went to the door we found someone had left a bag of fabrics on the doorstep!

Accepting, encouraging, caring

'The project is not about getting people on to college courses or anything like that, it's just accepting and encouraging and caring, positive input into people's lives. And if their goal is to get to work, that's fine, but because of that we're very careful where we go for our funding. There's a lot of funding available for deprived areas, but the government want figures, how many people do you get through the door, how many people have you got back to work – there's a lot of pressure and we don't want to put pressure on people who come here because they've got so much pressure in their own lives. It's almost like an escape – they're going to be valued here for who they are – not as a mother or a wife or a daughter, it's a place where they can come and they can enjoy an input for themselves and be encouraged. But funding doesn't seem to be a problem for us – praise God!'

Structure of the project

The Lighthouse has just applied for charitable status, so they have gone through the process of being vetted by the Charities Commission. They now have a very formal structure that has been established over two years. Having started with the idea of a coffee morning, they have been on an incredibly steep learning curve and now have a board of trustees, who are responsible for the overall structure and policies and improvements. Below that is Catherine as the development manager of the project: she is responsible to the local steering group which oversees the running of this Centre, and if they open another Centre it will have its own steering group. These are made up of different members of the community, there is someone from the health service, a local teacher, somebody who works with the local youth, somebody from the council offices, various members of the community, people who represent the church, and somebody who represents the big network of volunteers.

A co-ordinator looks after the day-to-day running of the Centre, and there is somebody for administration; they are in the process of documenting the structure, in order to move forward into opening another Centre. There are child facilities on the floor below, a fully qualified registered play group, so mums can come with children from just 12 months old and access all the activities going on in the Centre. 'Which is wonderful,' said Catherine, 'because I think for children from 12 months to school age, when they're mobile and you have to do everything with them, to be able to have a couple of hours respite and do something that is productive for yourself, is wonderful.'

Blackheath next

'We've started negotiations with the local community at Blackheath, which is the next town, and we're gathering a portfolio of support for that Centre. We're thrilled – we have a complete group of the entire churches of every congregation in Blackheath who have come together to support the opening of a new Centre in that area. That says a lot for the community, because often they are so separated, aren't they? But they've all come together to support the Centre. I'm not sure when that will be opening, but it will be sometime in the next 12 months.

Why the Lighthouse?

'The name comes from Matthew 5.14: "You are the light of the world", the light shining in the community. But what the lighthouse symbolizes is the light shining to help people avoid crashing on the rocks of life. So it's a perfect name in every way. In the first few weeks we were lucky to get anyone through the door, for a number of reasons – because they were unsure who we were, what we were trying to do, and also because we're a Christian project. We're not an evangelistic project at all, but we're openly Christian and some people asked, "Do you have to believe in God to come here?" It was quite difficult – some people thought we were just going to preach to them or we would be getting out the Bible and praying.

'So we had to get over that and the numbers were quite slow at the beginning, but in a seven-week period at the beginning we had about 250 people through the door, and then 12 months later in the same period we had about 600, and for the same period in this year, our second year, I think we've had about 1200, so it's moving along nicely. That isn't 1200 different people because at some point during the process people come every day. It's just wonderful to see that from the beginning when people say, "Oh, no, I don't want anything, I'm just happy with my coffee", the desire inside them grows and it's like a sponge and they can't get enough of it, and they want to come every day and join in whatever is going on. I would say we have about 15 or 20 people in a day, we think that's a nice number.

Time to chat

'We're about befriending, not about numbers, it's about the quality of services that we offer. We just want enough time to talk, we like to sit with people and have a cup of coffee and see how things are going, so we can get to know people and their difficulties. If there were a lot of people we wouldn't be able to do that. They are people mainly from the estate, but some come from the surrounding areas. And we get people from backgrounds that are not deprived at all, but struggling. We've got one lady who comes quite frequently, she's a nurse. Her husband's out all day from seven to seven, and she's got a young baby who's really quite difficult, crying an awful lot. And this lady's a career woman, and now she's at home all day, every day, with this little baby crying all the time. Now she's just as much in need as anybody else of stimulating company, and she said to me that she feared where she was heading, psychologically, because she was going out of her mind at home.

'So people are in need in all sorts of ways, and I don't think it's got a lot to do with what you've got in the bank or your financial circumstances. So we bring in anyone that walks in the door, anyone is welcome. And if they've walked through the door and made it to the stairs, they will have some need or other, we don't always find out straightaway, because we don't automatically say, "Well, what have you come for?" We just accept people in and we get to know them, and one day they may feel like sharing whatever they're struggling with. We can help them. It's on a very subtle level.

You can do loads of things

'I think once you've established what your problem is, and are ready to take the step to do something about it, you're halfway there. But a lot of people are struggling and they're not sure why, because they think that's life, that's how it is, and nobody cares anyway, so I may as well get on with it. If people have got to that point, and if they've adopted a sort of victim mentality, "Well, this is how my mum lived, and this is how her mum lived before her", they come from a very dysfunctional background, and that's just how life is. And it doesn't have to be that way. But people like that won't know it, they won't have realized that life can be full and exciting. Even if you haven't got a lot of money, and with kids tottering along behind you, you can still achieve a lot for yourself, personal goals, instead of going through life feeling the victim of your circumstances, just a drudge in your home environment.

Fulfilling potential

'It's a wonderful thing to see people's lives changing – their whole body language, their posture, their expressions, it's wonderful. When they first come in, a lot of people sit in a corner, they've got their coffee and they're sort of hiding behind the cup, and you try and talk to them and it's, "I'm all right". And then, like Jo for example, she came every day, and soon she was taking over the office! She would come into my office and say, "You're not doing that right, you should be doing this", telling me what to do, and wanting to run the show, and I just think, that's wonderful. (Jo revealed great mathematical ability and is now studying to become a maths teacher.) We've all got that potential, and that's what God wants for us, to live the fullness of life. It's difficult, because I so often think, "Oh, if you knew the Lord, his peace and his love in your life and in your heart, life would be so different for you because you'd have hope, no matter where you are." But we're not about preaching the gospel here. If people ask about our beliefs and why we do what we do, then we're allowed to say, but we have a strict policy on not sharing our belief unless we're asked. But people have come to know God through the project, which is fantastic.

The power of people speaking together

'It's very powerful when a number of people come together speaking with the same voice. This is one of the things that the Lighthouse has been instrumental in getting off the ground. We have one lady who's been awakened into changing the immediate environment. She has become chairperson of the tenants' association, and through her, a lot of money has come through the council for improvement, and the people have realized that they can actually do something about their environment. It's exciting. (I keep on saying it's exciting – at all my meetings I'm known for saying, "This is so exciting, and that's so exciting!")

Terrible drug problems

'We're having camera security systems put in, and I think about £150,000 is going into improving the estate. Vandalism is so rife, we have terrible drug problems here. We have about five dealers living on the estate. There are only 500 houses, so that's quite a lot of dealers. People find used syringes everywhere. There's a lot of grassy areas, but you never see a child playing out, because it's not safe. People leave syringes deliberately in places where you will get caught by one, on banister rails, facing the wrong way, so that it will go into you. We have to be very careful when we're dropping leaflets and things – we have to have a man with us and go in twos. It's staggering really, because you look out of the window and actually it looks quite pleasant. But it's very difficult, particularly for the people who live in the blocks where dealers live, because they get a lot of people coming in and out because of their trade, and then using the communal areas as toilets. People have to bring their children through. So some of the money is going to go to more staff to help keep areas clean and safe.

'I sit on a forum, and the police are on it, crime prevention officers, social services, the rent office, the fire brigade (because they're always coming out), the tenants' association. Time and time again at those meetings the question of catching the dealers comes up. The police are aware who the dealers are, but every time they try and do a raid, there's nothing there. Every time. How people get to find out, I've no idea. If one dealer does get sent to prison another one moves in. We just try to make it more difficult for them to operate, and safer for the other tenants, and try to cut down on the petty crime and the vandalism, because of the cameras. We're making headway and people are awakening to realize that they can do something themselves in their own situation.

No play facilities

'One of the things that came from the tenants' association when we did a survey and asked what changes the tenants would like to see, is that there are no play facilities. All those homes, loads and loads of children, but no play facilities at all. So we set about raising money for a play area and we've raised £20,000, which is what it's going to cost to have a lovely bright play area built, just at the side of this building. We're hoping that the work will start in the spring. And of course it will be another communal area, for those who haven't yet ventured into the Lighthouse. We're just having a little picket fence, we can't have a high fence, but it's being covered by CCTV cameras.

Millennium award

'I was a recipient of a Millennium award at the beginning of the year, and there was an award ceremony, with 50 other awardees. I was staggered at all these people working on a voluntary basis in their communities, in so many ways and with such a passion for the work that they're doing for other people – caring and loving other people. How do you get across to your family and friends that this is more important than a healthy bank balance?'

(We were delighted to hear from Catherine that she has recently remarried. She is now Catherine Marshall.)

2

Single Parents Together

'My Kids & Me' was set up by single parents for single parents so we can help others who have suffered through breakdown in relationships, or just finding things hard. We offer support to others like ourselves and we value every individual who walks through the door whatever religion, colour, gender or disability. We arrange a low-cost annual holiday. We arrange trips out as a group. We can help you check your benefits. Our 24-hour support line can be used in an emergency, or just for a chat. (Group leaflet)

In the bright and welcoming premises of a church hall in Newcastle we met Joanne, the co-ordinator, several mums and children and two dads, Gary and Mick. Joanne and Gary were part of the group that started 'My Kids & Me' in August 1995. Gary is the chairperson: 'There were a lot of us in the same situation and where we were there wasn't a lot of facilities for what we wanted for our children. So we decided the best thing was to do it ourselves, get a place where the children could play together and be safe.' They started in a small church hall but soon outgrew it and with some trepidation took on the bigger commitment of St Peter's, with its good facilities and safe grassy space for the children to play outside. They pay St Peter's £3,000 a year for using the premises three times a week and feel that is very reasonable, since it also includes heating. They find the church very supportive in many ways, for instance not charging for the use of the hall for fundraising events. Funding is a constant worry, Gary told us. 'We've had a couple of small grants from the National Lottery. We began with a £500 start-up grant from SPAN (Single Parent Action Network) in Bristol. The Newcastle Voluntary Services

15

gave us a lot of information. And it snowballed from there. We started off in the red, we've got out of the red and since then we've stayed in the black. And because the parents think so much of the group, they've done a lot of fund-raising themselves – anything from a pub crawl in fancy dress to street collections, jumble sales, car boot sales, anything.'

The kids get on so well together – the parents too

We visited at a quiet time but when all the children are in, the whole building is full of activity. 'We try to keep the older ones in the top end, eight years old and over, and they can have their music. In the bottom end we try and do arts and crafts, computer games and board games. They enjoy that side of things as well,' Gary told us. He has four children and since they haven't seen their mother for a while, it's nice for them to have contact with some mums. Others don't see their dads much and like to see the four or five dads who come. 'The kids come here and they aren't picked on. Nobody says, "You haven't got a Mum" or "You haven't got a Dad". I can honestly say we've never had to really scold children for fighting. They don't do it. I think it's because they've gone through a crisis and they see that everybody else has gone through the same. And that works among the parents as well. So it makes it worthwhile at the end of the day. It's nice to see when somebody new comes in – we take them from a certain point and try to build them back up again and keep them going. They nearly always stay, so we think we must be doing something right!'

'This becomes their extended family'

Joanne explained that the majority of people who come to the group don't get support from their own extended families, for one reason or another. 'They may live somewhere else in the country, or they may not speak to them, being single parents. So what we tend to find is this becomes their family, their extended family. If they're having problems they ring each other up, and support each other as well. They don't just come here, they'll meet up in other places, maybe going for a drink or a weekend away sometimes, helping each other doing decorating or helping move house. Whatever's needed, there'll be somebody, at least one person with that kind of experience, who can give a hand, and I think that's where a lot of the bonding comes from, why we feel it's such an important place and such an important group to be involved in. They do strive to keep it going and they do strive to find the funds to make things happen.'

Gary stressed the importance of their 24-hour help line: 'They always know there's somebody they can get in touch with at any time. There's always somebody at the end of that telephone, 24 hours a day. If the person at the end of the telephone can't help, there's somebody within the group that can. We've taken families out at a crisis point and put them in a women's refuge or to Joanne's house, to make them safe.'

Debbie's story

That's exactly what happened to Debbie. She told us she had been in a violent relationship for 16 years and until she met the single parents' group and started reading about domestic violence she just took it for granted that married life was like that. 'I didn't even class myself as living in domestic violence. I thought it was just a way of life. He could have any woman he wanted, but I had to be there.' At one point Debbie had tried to commit suicide and she feels sure that if she had not met the group that is how she would have ended up. 'It wasn't till I was meeting other people and reading leaflets about the different ways of domestic violence and mind games and I thought, "He's done every one of them, and I didn't even realize, I just used to take it."' The group told her that whenever she wanted to get out they could take her to a safe place. At first she was too scared of what her husband might do if she left but after he had badly beaten her up, she thought, 'I can't take any more of it', and rang for the group to come and get her. 'While I was trying to get out, stupid me, I was hoovering up to leave the house tidy for him! So I went to the safe house with my three children – two safe houses actually. He found out where I was in one so they shifted me to another one. And then I got my own house and went up from there. When I met the group it just made me stronger.'

Gary told us what a good feeling it is, 'Taking someone when they're at their lowest and building them up and giving them back some self-confidence, so they realize they are a person who can continue on in life and, as Debbie said, going from somebody who was a carpet to someone who knows she is worthy of being a person. Now Debbie is planning to start her own group against domestic violence.'

The Open Door

Debbie told us that she has been awarded a Millennium grant of £2,600 to help her train and prepare to start her group. 'Hopefully I'll run it for one day a week in here on Thursdays, the only day it's not being used. I've got the name of it! Open Door. But I'm not going to call it for women in domestic violence, because women will not come into the group if it says domestic violence. I've found that out over the months I've been training and meeting other people. They've advised me, "I wouldn't add domestic violence." Because a lot of people stay in their homes and they won't even discuss it with anybody. But if it's just a normal women's group, they're more likely to come in and then sort things out once they're here.

'I've got a number of certificates behind me now. What I'm doing is, I just do any course I can, training, so I can get a certificate at the end of it, and make a portfolio. I want to be a support worker in domestic violence. It took me a long time to realize what I wanted to be. I couldn't find the name of what I actually wanted to be. I've still got a long way to go and things are still hard because I still get bits and pieces of trouble with my ex-husband.

'It's taken me three years to eventually get the children to live together without fighting. The oldest was always hit by her Dad, she was always hit and kicked and slapped. It's taken a lot but I think they're getting there. We're all getting there gradually – you sit down and you talk to them. Until recently I was like that. I was up in arms if anyone touched my kids or went for my kids. But I've calmed down now. Now I'd rather go and talk.

'The greatest thing of all, believe it or not, is I've got a bank account, a cheque book! I've never, ever had one. I just could not believe it!'

Joanne commented, 'It's something that you can control yourself. For 16 years you've had somebody else controlling everything you did. I think it was a big culture shock to you even to think that you had to make your own decisions.' Joanne explained to us that Debbie had had to start a house from two black bags, 'That's all she took out of the house when we took her out. She's had to literally start from scratch. To get three years down the road to where she is now, to the point where she is going to be a community support worker for domestic violence. She would never have thought of that three or four years ago.'

Training for parents

Debbie is not the only parent getting certificates. When the group asked the parents what they wanted to do (there is a management committee but things are run on a friendly basis and everybody has a say) the main thing they all wanted was training so that they could feel more confident as parents. Joanne told us that Jo Forster had set up the training with funds from the North West Partnership; the University for Industry provided the Fun With Kids element; Newcastle College provided the tutor and the BBC, who were running an Adult Education Promotion in conjunction with UFI, arranged the awards ceremony at the end of the course. Gary told us what the course had involved. 'There were four or five different categories. There was Fun with Kids, there was Parental Skills as in reading and writing with your children, basic education, there was First Aid Skills, Confidence Building. . . . They incorporated this into one big 16-week course, and it was held in the big hall here, so the parents felt comfortable with it because they knew the surroundings and they knew the people that were in it. And the trainer they sent was really good, she made everybody feel comfortable. We were the first national group to do this training and they've actually named the course after us, 'My Kids & Me'! At least ten or eleven of our parents were on the training and achieved certificates. It gives you back some self-respect and some confidence to see that you are worth something and you can achieve these things.'

Gary himself got a lot of new ideas out of the training. 'I hadn't realized that when you do cooking or cutting out or whatever with your children, or take them out, you are educating them, you're doing things right. I actually made a puppet for my kids. I would never have thought of doing something like that. You think it's not a manly thing to be doing – me stuck with bits of paper. It reminded me of Blue Peter. But nobody took the Michael out of me.'

Gary's story

We were very touched by the way Gary was able to see the break-up of his marriage from his wife's point of view. 'The way that I have come into this situation was that my wife went out to work when I didn't have a job and I was at home looking after our four children. And she gained a different lifestyle than what she had. So she realized she didn't want the family life, she had found a different life. She had her own wages and she had her own lifestyle and she decided she didn't want to be a parent any more. I think a lot of women have found a new life like that and realized they got married too early. I look at my marriage and I think maybe she did get married too early. She was 18 and I was 20. I had been working abroad and I had a sort of life where I'd done a lot of things but she had only lived in Newcastle and she went straight from school to work and then she had a family so she hadn't had a life. And then she found a life and it was a different lifestyle and she liked it and decided that was the way she was going to go. She was just there one day and gone the next.'

A lot of single dads

Mick, the other dad we met, was also looking after his kids while his wife went to work. He said he just woke up one morning and it was finished. There was no love there any more. According to Gary, 'There are a lot of single dads out there as well but a lot of them won't come forward. A lot of it is pride – they won't come forward and admit they're single parents. It's admitting you're a failure. To me at the time, it just felt like I had to be there for my children. It was hard to be mother and father but it was just the sort of thing you had to get on with.'

Supporting each other

'My Kids & Me' has built up a valuable base of knowledge and experience with which they support each other and help new members of the group. Joanne did training with social services in Newcastle around family support, 'I've had a lot of experience in what social workers should and shouldn't do, what they can and can't do, so that came in very helpful. I mean, we've had a social worker threaten to take a child off a mum because she was by herself in a women's aid refuge, but I know that Social Services recognize that women's aid refuges are safe places for children, so I couldn't understand why she was being threatened with this. So it was up to me to go and challenge this because obviously the mum didn't know. Once we challenged this, an apology came back and the social worker began doing her job as she should do. It's little things like that which make a significant difference.' They can tell people what their rights are, because how are people to know if nobody tells them? If one of the parents has to go to court there's always somebody who will go with them and support them. Sometimes they sit in on case conferences to do with children, perhaps if a child is being taken into care for some reason.

Because 'My Kids & Me' is not tied into a lot of bureaucracy they are always learning, always developing according to the needs and the ideas of the members. As Gary said, 'If somebody comes up with an idea, let's back that idea if it's workable and get moving with it. Not put anybody down, take people as they are, give them something to aim for and realize that they are worthy, too.' We were very happy to get a letter from Joanne some months after our visit, telling us, 'On Wednesday of this week the interviews that we did for the television was broadcast on ITV and we were all very excited. The coverage was very positive and we are now expecting more people to join us. We have also secured a grant to fund a Sunday service for single parents and their children so they can have a rest over the weekend. Sundays is one of the worst days for single parents because there is nothing for them to do and nowhere to go, so we now have the money to pay for crèche workers and we are also planning to have a Sunday lunch for the families who attend. So it is all very exciting!'

Combating isolation

'Isolation is a big downside to the single parent thing,' said Gary, 'because once you've put your children to bed you're in your house alone till the next day and a lot of the parents say that's very hard. We've had some social nights and some of them said it was the first time they'd had an evening out for years.' Often the children suffer from isolation too. For the smaller ones coming to the group is often their first opportunity to socialize with other children and enjoy being able to play outside. It is not just that many of them live in flats without gardens, it is that children face so many dangers out of doors on the estates.

We chatted about how much more restricted children's lives have become and Pam commented, 'What we and our neighbours were allowed to do as children, I wouldn't allow my children to do. I went out from first thing in the morning with jam sandwiches and a bottle of pop and came back for my tea and my mum never seemed to fret. I'd been to the local park or I'd gone for a bike ride. I wouldn't let mine out of sight. I wouldn't let her off the estate where I live and there's even some parts of my estate I wouldn't allow her on, because there's drug addicts, dealers . . .'; Emma added, 'You don't know whether somebody's molested children', and Sharon complained, 'My neighbour's children put my windows out. And their mother just sat on the side and let them get on with it.'

So access to safe space and varied activities is invaluable. 'We try to give them new experiences,' Joanne told us. 'Mick used to do catering for the airport, so over Christmas he decided to organize a three-course meal and 49 parents and children came. Some of the children hadn't experienced having more than one course put in front of them at any one meal, and they said, "I've just had my dinner – what's this?"' The annual caravan holidays at a campsite in Scarborough, in a big friendly group, have also been wonder-fully enriching experiences for both parents and children.

Struggling against stereotypes

All the parents feel they constantly face negative attitudes because of the bad publicity single parents have been getting over the last few years. 'None of the people here have chosen to become a single parent,' insists Joanne. 'Because of circumstances beyond their control that's just the situation they find themselves in. But the stereotype is, "It was your choice, you got yourselves into it, it's your fault." Even when we do our street collections, if people ask you what the collection's for and you say a single parents' group, some of them turn away because they immediately think, "Well, you've done it yourselves so we're not going to help you."'

'And one day,' pointed out Debbie, '*they* could be single parents, they don't know what's going to happen next week.'

We got talking about the government's New Deal for getting single parents back to work or into education and all agreed that the problem of childcare was the greatest obstacle, especially when children get sick. Joanne had learned that in other European coun-tries single parents can get up to 20 days' leave when a child is sick whereas here, if you have no extended family to help, you can end up losing your job because a crèche or a childminder won't take a sick child. 'If we could go back to work with decent child care, we would do that, but we don't see why we should have to put up with sub-standard services just because we're single parents.'

Teenage mums

We asked Joanne whether any teenagers who've had babies join the group and she explained that girls under 25 come under the Children and Young People's section and are looked after by the Social Services. But they all know plenty of teenage mums and had illuminating thoughts about the problem. Joanne feels strongly that, 'It's not a lot of help to a teenager when they keep reading about sex and being on the pill and condoms and all that. That isn't going to help them because what they're not being taught is the emotional stress and strains that come with having a sexual relationship – they don't know anything about that. What they need is teaching about the varieties of life, about having self-worth for themselves, because they're not going to go and get pregnant unless they feel insecure, unless they feel undermined or they have no self-esteem. You just wouldn't do it, once you know in yourself that you're a person in your own right, you wouldn't allow anybody to violate you like that. It's only when you become vulnerable . . .'

This is how it's going to be

Emma felt that girls do need practical information about sex and about what caring for a baby actually entails. 'What they're really longing for when they have a baby is unconditional love, but a teenager just doesn't see the whole picture – I didn't when I had Nicole. You've got this baby, which is so gorgeous and you fall in love with it straight away but when they're toddlers getting into everything it's a different kettle of fish. If someone had come into my school and said, "This is how it's going to be, up every three hours during the night feeding it, tied all the time, you can't run out of milk and go down the shops . . ." I'd have had a totally different idea.'

'That actually says a lot about your own family life,' responded Joanne, 'how you were brought up, how insecure you must have felt within your own family. You weren't loved, or didn't have the affection that really you should have got. When I fell pregnant with my boy it was something that I didn't particularly want to do, but I certainly didn't think it was a disaster. Again it was about my own childhood, where the insecurities were, the lack of love and affection, because there wasn't any in my family. I could focus on my own child and pour out to him all those things that I never got. Young girls think, "Yes, that's the unconditional love I want", but if they're 16 when they have the baby, when they're 18 and they want to go out with their friends that's when they start the regrets. If they've got the support, fine, but if the support's not there, things can happen, they can start to neglect their child themselves. You really need to look at their family background, where they've been, what effect it's had on them, because you just wouldn't, if you had your own self-worth and confidence in your own ability you just wouldn't allow yourself to be used and abused like that. You really wouldn't.'

If there's no hope, there's no future

Self-worth and empowerment are what 'My Kids & Me' is all about. Joanne summed it up for us, 'We don't judge anybody in here. We're all sitting here and we're all on the same level, and it doesn't matter what's happened in your past, what you've done. You could be the best shoplifter in Newcastle, it doesn't matter. At the end of the day, when you're here you're the same as everybody else, and if you have problems and we can help, we will, and if we can't help we can find somebody who can. It's about not judging people as they come through the door. We've got on our leaflets that we value everybody that comes in, because we know they might come in at a crisis point, but we've all come in with our own gifts, and if we can tap into those gifts, then it has to be strength for all, and that's what we aim at. Everybody's got to have hope, or it's not worth living.'

❧ 3 ❧

Leaven in the Community

Women like these act as leaven in their communities in endless ways, responding to the needs they see around them: children in difficult family situations; the loss of community spirit; the problems of asylum seekers. Some are trying, through projects like RAP and Heartstone, to inspire children and young people to become 'leaveners' in their communities.

RESCUING CHILDREN

Meeting Pat McKinnon, we thought the 74 children she had fostered had been very lucky. Now happily remarried, she has three grown-up children from a difficult first marriage (and some grandchildren) and has adopted three ex-foster-children: Dawn, her brother Christopher and Chardene, all from painful backgrounds but now doing very well – Dawn had just been chosen as Head Girl of her school. They are all active in the life of Salford Cathedral.

Very Victorian

Pat came from a family of 16 children, the older ones having to look after the younger. 'Mum was always in the kitchen and we were only allowed just outside the door, no wandering about. We knew our duties and we did them and that kept Mum happy. But when you get a bit older, if somebody gives you a little bit of a time, it's head over heels! I married at 18 – far too young. And then I still wasn't allowed out! I wanted to be with the children anyway but now I tell Dawn not to rush into anything – she's got all her life before her. Later I became manageress at a cake shop. Children came in whose mothers were so free with their hands and yelling at them. I'd give them sweets and pay up at the end of the day to make the till right. Good job it wasn't my shop!'

'Foster parents wanted'

Pat's love and concern for children later led her, after thorough consultation with all her family, to answer an advertisement for foster parents and so began her long career as a foster mother. 'It's marvellous to see them growing up. Some of them are very sad, you don't like some of them to go back [to their parents] because you get them blossoming, and the next thing is, unfortunately, the courts say, "No, they have got to go back", and that breaks your heart, knowing they're going back to what you rescued them from. When you hear some of the children's stories, it breaks your heart to think what some people can put children through.' Pat has seen every kind of family breakdown and feels that the modern job situation bears much responsibility for it.

'You're my Mum now'

Dawn and Christopher were from a family of six, all frequently in care, the parents with drink problems. Dawn arrived with severe burns and Christopher like a little bird always opening his mouth for food. 'Big tall thing he is now, he's gorgeous.' Chardene, 'a gem, a wonderful child', was put into care one Friday evening so that her single mum could go out with her friends. 'They brought her to me, and mum never came back for her. Several years later when Social Services did find her and asked her about the child, she shrugged, "Oh, I thought she'd have been adopted." I only know that she's a beautiful woman. I tell Chardene, "Your Mum's beautiful and you're beautiful." "Don't talk about that, Mum," she says, "you're my Mum now." Christopher doesn't remember being anywhere else but I think Dawn's got things on her mind that eventually will come out. At the moment she's doing very well, and I just leave that up to my prayers. I think eventually she'll understand why these things happen. But they do feel different from other children. I tell them, "When other children have a go at you, just say, 'Well, I'm very special because I've got two Mums and two Dads. And my Mum chose me.'" I love them to bits.'

STALWART AMID THE WRECKAGE OF THE TEAMS

Bernadette Askins, the Ecumenical Officer of the Roman Catholic Diocese of Hexham and Newcastle, arranged our programme in the North East, and took us first to The Teams area of Gateshead, where we had a room in the presbytery of Holy Rosary Church – by kindness of the parish priest, Father Bill Rook – for our conversation with two women who were very active in the life of the church: Chrissie Bate, a widow with three children, and Margaret Robson, who was divorced and had one son. They gave us a survey of the history of the area, from the Jarrow March, through the miners' strike, to the building of the motorway and the subsequent redevelopment and destruction of the old community.

On the loss of traditional employment, Chrissie said, 'There used to be the paper mill, the rope works, the glass works, the steel – well, the steel works are still there, but not like it used to be – and the gas works, and the flour mill, and the soap works.' To Pamela's question, 'And what's replaced all that?' Chrissie's answer was, flatly, 'Nothing.' Margaret added, 'You've got the Metrocentre now, that provides a lot of jobs, but they're part-time jobs for women and they're very badly paid. And you've got to pay to get there, of course.' Chrissie remembered, 'It was a good shopping area, shops up both sides of the road. There used to be a little shop, Charlton's – she used to sell everything, your doormats to your paraffin. . . . And she knew people by name. Now you've got to go to Gateshead, Newcastle or the Metrocentre.'

It was, however, the building of the motorway that really changed The Teams and cut it in half. 'I think everybody would say the motorway has demolished The Teams community,' said Margaret. 'If you look at a map you'll see The Teams split in two. You used to know all the families, you grew up with each other, but in the other estate they've come from all over, so you're sort of like strangers. I've been there 22 years so you start to get into each other's ways, but at first it was starting all over again, everybody was strangers.' Chrissie added, 'There's quite a lot moved out, older neighbours, so you don't know the younger ones, you just sort of see them passing where before you knew everyone by their Christian name and you knew their surname.'

Community Care, however, seemed to have the right idea. 'They do shopping and what not,' said Margaret, 'and they have a luncheon club twice a week. In fact a lot of people say the old people are really well catered for in The Teams.' Chrissie added, 'My daughter works there, in the Community Centre. They collect them, take them down for their dinner, and those ones that don't want to go, they bring their dinner out to them. And they take people away to the baths for exercises, they collect you from home and they take you back. So you're meeting people and you're getting out.' But to Marigold's question, 'What is there for young people to do around here?' the answer was again a flat 'Nothing.'

The Community Development worker, Pat Devlin, like so many of the women we spoke to, had started something that was a sign of hope, as Margaret could testify. 'There's the community business, a launderette and a little café at the back. It was trying to create employment for the people in The Teams. It was Pat Devlin's brainwave. She was the one that pulled it all together.'

FROM SOMALIA TO ROEHAMPTON

We met Zahra Ali, a 31-year-old Muslim woman from Somalia, through our friend Jane Sherwin, now helping asylum-seekers through Churches Together in the Roehampton area. Zahra has lived there for nearly a year, after five in Manchester and two in Streatham, and has made a home for her husband and three young children.

'Of course I speak English!'

Zahra went into labour with her first child just 16 days after arriving in Britain, with no medical records to help the doctor, but all went well. The day after the birth a nurse came to tell her it was lunchtime and, seeing from her chart what a new arrival Zahra was, just pointed to her mouth and then to the door and said, 'You, lady, out!'

'Are you talking to me?' said Zahra, sending the nurse into shock!

'Oh, my God, you speak English!'

'Of course I speak English. It's an international language, I finished university in English back home. Why didn't you just ask me?'

But Zahra much appreciates the NHS and also the friendliness of English people.

Back home her mother would have done everything for her and at first Zahra found coping on her own hard. 'The first day I didn't even know how to use the nappies. Three days after I left hospital I had to go shopping, because I didn't have any food at home. I was nearly in tears, saying, "What have I done to deserve this, straight from the hospital to go shopping?" But if I send my husband to go shopping, if I ask for salad he will buy cabbage! So in a year you become a very experienced mum.'

Helping the Somali community

During her eight years in the UK Zahra has tried very hard to help the Somali community. She has been a link worker for the City Council, a bilingual assistant teacher, visiting women in hospital, but always coming up against tribal prejudice and traditional attitudes to women. 'If you don't accept or believe in tribes you don't have many friends. When you meet somebody, the first question they ask is "What tribe are you?" When you tell them, they maybe don't like that tribe, so they won't make friends.' Zahra had moved from Manchester for this reason, and found there were more communities in London and less tribalism.

She is now studying to become a nurse but is also a part-time volunteer helping Somali pupils in an ESOL course at South Thames College, Roehampton, and in her daughter's primary school.

In a man's world

Zahra's keenness to study and get on earned her the criticism of her fellow-countrymen, who asked her why she wasn't content to stay at home and be a wife. 'I say, "I'm doing the best I can, I'm not doing it for you, I'm doing it for myself." And they say, "No, you are a woman, you are a wife and a mum, why don't you just stay at home, clean and cook?" And I say, "I do that, but still I have a lot of time." Back home we live in a man's world, and they want the same here. I'm doing the best I can to become what I am.' We left full of admiration for Zahra's courage in standing up for her convictions.

RAP COMMUNITY ACTION, OXFORD

RAP (Right Angle Productions) is based in East Oxford in an old industrial building covered with children's bright murals. Their leaflet explains:

> RAP uses participatory video methods to give young people the confidence and the means of expression for anything they feel strongly about. We encourage a more active role in the community through the ideas of Agenda 21, looking at issues like sustainability, recycling, making a better environment to live in both in appearance and in reality.

In this millennium year, RAP is participating in On the Line, working with five communities in Oxford in the project set up by Oxfam, Channel 4 and WWF-UK to celebrate countries on the Meridian line. They will be taking part in a touring multi-media exhibition in December 2000.

Marigold, who has close links with Quakers in Cuba, met Katie Beinart and Jo Huyg of RAP at an event where they were showing the video they had made with children in Havana. She later went to their base to learn about their work with disadvantaged children in East Oxford.

Making a difference to children – children making a difference

'We hand over the project to the young people so they can take it in any direction they want to,' explained Jo. 'We just use the camera to start to talk about issues, for them to look at their area and discuss things going on. Also to be proud of their area and realize they can make a difference.' They try to get the kids to go more deeply into local issues. Katie felt that some environmental projects for children are just single issue campaigns like a rubbish clearing day, but they don't look at the underlying problems like why we've got a lot of waste, and what about recycling.

After getting used to the camera by making a film of each child saying their name and something about where they live, the kids do a mapping exercise, talking about things on the map and places they like or dislike. They go and film interviews with local people, then come back and watch the film and discuss issues arising from it and action they might take.

RAP does one-off projects in schools or youth groups but they much prefer long-term projects like the RAP Club for local kids where they can get to know them really well and do all sorts of activities as well as the video work. 'Because the youth service provision in this area is not very good,' Jo continued, 'we started doing sessions for just any kids off the street, so quite a few of the boys who used to just hang around the youth club, where there was nothing going on, started joining in. The RAP Club has an allotment – we were there last night for two and a half hours! The kids just go mad for it. And a really important aspect of our work is just going out and having fun outside, running around and climbing trees or playing in the river.'

RAP was started by Nick Lunch and is run as a co-operative. Nick, Katie and Jo (helped by some volunteers) work all hours with the different groups (including a group of young asylum-seekers, mainly Kosovans and Kenyans) and find it very rewarding but quite stressful. The kids confide in them as friends and that sometimes puts a weight of responsibility on them. Jo said, 'You can't just think about something and say that's over and done with, it's all in your head.' Katie explained that they have a management committee, including a highly experienced youth worker who acts as a mentor when needed. But the worries are outweighed by the enjoyment and development experienced by the young people. 'That's what's really nice about it', said Katie, 'they turn up because they want to be there – no one's forcing them into it.'

FOLLOWING A THREAD FROM LINCOLN
TO DINGWALL VIA INDIA

One weekend Marigold happened to visit Lincoln Cathedral and in a side aisle found a small exhibition featuring a beautiful textile/mixed material banner made by three girls from the Birchwood Youth Centre. Its theme was remembrance of the Holocaust and the danger of anti-Semitism today. Very impressed, Marigold wrote to Birchwood and learned that Kelly Hammond, Mellissa Peech and Vicki Fish, advised by art worker Lucy Jackson, had designed and made the banner as part of the Heartstone Project, Heartstone being 'a campaigning organization which works to encourage young people to challenge issues of oppression and intolerance'. The evaluation of the project, kindly sent to us by Birchwood youth worker Denise Benetello, told us that after studying and discussing the 'pack' provided by Heartstone, 'the young people undertook some research into the rise of anti-Semitism and the Holocaust and made comparisons with what was currently happening in Kosovo. This took the form of visiting the local library, watching a video about the concentration camp at Treblinka, looking at old photographs, and studying current newspapers and news reports.' The girls were inspired to depict what they had seen in their banner and proclaimed, 'This piece of work is a testament to all the people in the world who are oppressed and persecuted because of their race, creed, religion or colour.' The banner formed part of a Heartstone Exhibition in York Minster in November 1999, which was shown again at the European Parliament in Brussels in November 2000.

Marigold then followed the thread (telephonically!) to Dingwall to learn more about Heartstone from its moving spirit, Sitakumari, an Indian dancer. The story of the Heartstone Odyssey was first told during a long train-ride from Bombay to Madras in 1985 and through Sitakumari was published here as an inspiring story for children. Children responded not only with enjoyment but by wanting to do something positive about the issues raised so poignantly within the engrossing narrative. 'So no one planned Heartstone, it came into being because its time had come,' said Sitakumari. The project now produces a whole range of materials designed to say to young people, like the Birchwood girls, 'What does this spark off in you?' Some 2,000 schools around the country are now involved and the project's work and methodology are supported by Sheffield, Exeter and London universities. There are also ever-increasing international links.

Sitakumari herself dances to promote Heartstone, as well as directing operations from the Heartstone office in Dingwall. She stresses that the aim is to combat intolerance in all contexts, for example within communities, as well as between communities. Some of her own experience is reflected, she says, in *Chandra's Story*, which forms the first part of *The Heartstone Odyssey*.

It is impressive and touching to read the letters and poems in which many young participants express what the Heartstone Project has meant to them. Samantha, a mixed-race girl who took part in a dance project, wrote: 'For once in my life I feel special. Instead of just correcting [the words people use], I have actually helped make them stop and watch the performance and listen to what was being said by taking part myself. Whether or not they came just to watch their sons or daughters perform does not bother me because I know that while they were in the cathedral they got that message and stopped to think what the project was about.'

❦ 4 ❦

'A Table in the Wilderness'

THE FURNIVAL PUB-CHURCH

On a huge run-down housing estate in Sheffield we met Baptist minister Jane Grinonneau, through Marigold's friend Frances Morgan who is a volunteer at the Furnival, a public-house church with a wonderful collection of people and possibilities. Jane was Associate Minister at Northfield Baptist Church, Birmingham, from 1991 to 1996, when she became minister at the Furnival public-house church in the Sheffield Inner City Ecumenical Mission. She is also a part-time tutor at the Urban Theology Unit. Her account of her work in Birmingham, 'City Kids as Signs of the Kingdom', is published in *British Liberation Theology, Gospel from the City* (C. Rowland and J. Vincent (eds), Urban Theology Unit).

The front door takes you straight into the bright, cheerful café where everyone is made welcome. Behind that is the meeting room/church and down in the basement, as well as a TV and games room there is the colourful room in which Sister Una Burke of La Sainte Union works with children excluded from school. Unfortunately Sister Una was away during our visit but we were hosted by Sister Pat Daly in the house they share, and heard a lot about their multifarious activities in the community.

A history of the Furnival

'The story begins in the 1970s', Jane told us, 'when Sheffield's decline began as the steel industry became more mechanized. Many people were leaving the area and by the early 90s the nearby Methodist chapel's congregation was down to four. They couldn't afford to maintain the premises in spite of running a furniture refurbishing project in the cellar and finally they sold the premises to a housing association. They got an architect to draw up plans to build a hall for worship, where they could continue to have the lunch club, and maybe do some work with children and parents, but everything they tried failed. Early in 1996 Tetley's put this pub up for auction, because they weren't even able to sell enough beer, which says something about the poverty in the area! And the group of four Methodists, whose combined ages were just under 300 years, came in here and sat in the other room and experienced this auction. The asking price went up and up, and at £49,500 they said, "Well, we'll buy it." They had no money, and if you say at an auction that you'll buy something, you have a legal obligation to see that through. And they hadn't the money. So there was a phenomenal amount of work done until about May 22 when it became theirs. But between it becoming Methodist-owned property and Tetley relinquishing it, the vandals came in and seriously gutted the building, they took out all the equipment, took the boiler out of the cellar, so it was flooded, the curtains went from the windows, all the furnishing went.

Seeking guidance from God

'We opened the place in September 1996, and there was just Ann and Frank, Jack and Mary. I had felt very keenly early in the year that my pastorate in Birmingham was ending. I had pursued with the church in Manver Street, Bath, a very nice area, whether God wanted me there. I went through the six months' process of negotiating with the church and being interviewed. Then I went there for the weekend and at the end of it I felt that despite all the negotiations and agreement God did not want me at Manver Street. In the January, when I was up here from Birmingham doing a course of study at the Urban Theology Unit, I came round the area and felt immediately at home. I stood on the piazza outside and heard God say to me, "This is next, and you will live here, in this notorious block of flats." So I met the famous four and they said, "Well, we've no money, and we've no manse, and we've nothing", so I said, "Well, if it is of God, all these things will be found or it will be made possible." And I said to God, "If this really is what you want, could you give me a sign?" I was interviewed by a guy I'd never met before, representing Barnabas Charitable Trust. He and his wife interviewed me and they said, "Well, we really do feel that you're God's woman for this piece of work here", and after the hour and a half he said, "We will give you £6,000 for three years, so that you have a chance to see if this is what God wants." Well, if God wanted to drop me a memo, short of a first-class stamp, it seemed to be the sign. I knew I could live on £6,000 a year.

'What are those **** church people doing in our place?'

'The local community was initially hostile, including Josie Stocks, who now runs the café. At my induction in September 1996, she and the local people were looking and thinking, "What are those **** church people doing in our place? We'll get rid of them." And of course they might well have done if they'd chosen to. You will notice that the windows haven't got shutters, there are no bars on the windows. Apart from a couple of weeks ago when some local kids high on cannabis tried putting a paving stone through the window, we've had no vandalism on the outside at all. Which makes sense, because they know it's Josie's place, and Josie's theirs, it's their place.' (Josie would soon tell us her own story.)

Listening

'Since then,' continued Jane, 'we've just been listening and listening to what people wanted, what people were saying they needed. And overwhelmingly people wanted skills, they wanted jobs, they wanted to access hope, they wanted a meeting place, somewhere they could eat, they wanted something done about the kids excluded from school, they wanted something done about single parents and the youngsters. And interestingly in public meetings people were saying "We want a spiritual place where we can go and pray, a place of quiet." Nothing to do with denominations. So really the local people, through these public meetings that we went to, set the agenda, which I would have said just made visible to us God's agenda, addressing the issues of injustice and oppression that are here. And God has been amazing.

Josie and others – God's gifts

'And so in the three years God's gift has come to us in Josie and in many other people, so the resources have multiplied. The congregation, the faith community, is now 18, and people who had given up the church have found God, through the experience of what they found here, which has been a costly loving journey, you know? So the biblical picture is nothing clever, but yeast in the dough, not to make the bread like the yeast, for goodness sake, but for the yeast to be lost in the dough, or in the context of this place. What we're seeing is people experiencing their resurrection, coming up out of the horrors that this place does to people, to find a new beginning.'

Josie's story

Josie is a bit reserved but every now and then her face lights up in a beautiful smile. Hers is certainly a story of resurrection. She told us how she had been on drugs and had survived by shoplifting, for which she had been to prison three times. She and her friends had been horrified when they heard that their pub was going to become a church. 'When we first found out it was going to be a church we said, "No chance!" I was the first to sign a petition for it not to be a church. Then I started coming to church with my kids, just for a laugh. After a couple of weeks I started to listen to the stories and I didn't find it funny any more.' Josie told us that she worked in the kitchen in prison, but this is the first real paid job she's had. So she understands what life is like for the local kids. 'If it weren't for this place, I don't know, I'd probably be back inside. I didn't know what love was before, I thought people loved me because they'd say, "Here Josie, come and do this Social Services book for me" – I used to do it for them, to get a tenner out of it. They all used to come to me and I used to think, "Well, these are my mates, these are", but they weren't really, they were just using me. I've got true friends here now. If it weren't for this place I know, definitely, I'd be elsewhere.'

But if it weren't for Josie . . .

Jane told us that it is because the local people know that Josie is the manager of the café that it has become considered a safe place. 'I recognize that working alongside Josie, Josie being here, helps us to learn what we need to be doing, what God wants us to do, in a way that, without Josie, we couldn't do.'

When Josie first started working at the Furnival, and the local people saw Jane and the volunteers going in and out, they would say to Josie, 'We'll have to watch her.' Josie would tell them, 'You don't have to watch her for owt.' 'She's a police informer', they would say. 'If anybody came in they'd not seen before,' Josie said, 'they'd run in and say, "Is that CID?" and I'd say, "No, it's not", because I would tell them if the police were coming here. I would tell them a couple of days before, because I get to know whoever is coming in here. And I do say to kids, "Be careful because the police will be in here today. They're not in about you, it's for a meeting, it's not about you kids." Then they feel safe and they still hang about. I always tell them beforehand. If they just saw the police coming they'd run away.'

Saving someone special

Both Jane and Josie were still desperately sad about what had happened to a young girl a few days before. 'A little girl, 16 years old,' Josie told us, 'had been holding drugs, you know, for a big man. She started selling it and getting £20 a day. Then she got arrested last week, got picked up with £4,000 worth of crack – she's been locked up ever since. She run away Tuesday night from a secure unit. She came and stayed at a friend's house. I had to take her back, I didn't want to but I had to for her own sake. Now she's been sent away to a top security place, she's 16 years old. It weren't her thing, but that's what's happening round here, nowt for kids to do. I couldn't have done it a few years ago. I'd probably have hidden her away and got done meself.' Because Josie has shared similar experiences she was able to persuade the girl to go back, which Jane felt *she* would never have been able to do: 'I could say things, and I'm sure she knows I love her, but she couldn't hear me.

She could hear Josie because she knew where Josie's words were coming from, were out of her own experience and love.'

'Nobody can resist love'

Jane continued, 'Josie is a living message. People that know her hear and see the love of God. In church we just talk about it, package it up in statements and beliefs, and people say "Oh, I don't fancy that." But nobody can resist love. You can keep loving and, OK, it can be thrown away, but eventually people think, "I'm OK." That's what they need, isn't it? They've been rubbished by the system. They've been told, "Because you can't achieve in school, you're no good. Because you can't get a job, you're no good." So they get into the drugs scene. That way they've got money, and they say, "Now I can buy things I'm OK." It's the judgement we judge our kids with. It's not theirs, it's ours, it's our society's, we pull people down. I think that's what people who say they know God should be doing, challenging these things that hold people down, that put a 16-year-old girl down for four years because she's been found with stuff on her that belongs to some big powerful guy driving around in a car. He's untouchable, because he's got power, whereas a little lassie . . .'

'These kids just break your heart'

Jane described how tough life is in the area because the opportunities are never there. 'Opportunities to get jobs aren't there, because people in the main round here have not been well served by the education system. There aren't any resources in the area, there's no bank, no launderette. You wouldn't have realized coming up in the train, but Sheffield is all hilly, so if you've got a heart problem or you're not very mobile, like Josie's Mum who's not well, or if you've got kids in a pram, you're stuck, because you've got to push downhill or walk uphill. Bus fares are expensive, it's 50p to get on a bus to get from here down to the market. Where do you learn the skills, where do you have an opportunity to begin believing in yourself? It's two bus rides out to college. Josie will tell you stories of the kids who tried to have a go at college.'

According to Josie the local kids don't want to go to college, they want to come to the Furnival. 'I have somebody coming here to see me once a week. I've just done my Word Power/Skill Power, to do with catering. I've just been presented by the Lord Mayor with an Adult Learner of the Year Award. Now I'm going to do an NVQ [National Vocational Qualification] Level 2. Somebody comes here, I don't have to go out to college. And that's what the kids round here want, they don't want to travel to colleges.'

Jane has been trying to persuade the education authorities to organize that kind of thing. 'This is something I've learnt since I've been here. You'd think the answer would be to get some transport, get a minibus, and take the kids to wherever. But, no, it's too far, it's like saying to you, "Just pop to the moon for the afternoon." So we've been working quite hard, we've had millions of meetings, trying to get the people in power to see that in areas like this where there is no flowering, there is no opportunity, it's up to the people with the opportunities and the power to bring those opportunities where people are, not expect the people to go where they are.

'We're getting nearer and nearer; I'm really hopeful that Josie might start her course this autumn, but it's about getting people to spend their budgets differently, so that rather than saying, "Well, if we're going to run this course, we need at least ten people", we say, "No, no, no, if you've got one key neighbourhood person, one key local woman, then you resource a local person." Local people trust Josie, then Josie will say, "Why don't you come and do this course in the café?" We're looking at doing something at the end of the café day, then people can come into a place that is theirs with Josie, because they know Josie's safe, and Josie's OK, because Josie's done it, so if Josie can do it, it must be real.'

Plans for the future

A credit union is already under way and there is a volunteer who comes in once a week to give people advice about money matters. 'We've managed to do a deal with the city,' Jane told us, 'to get the lease of three shops nearby that they were going to pull down because they're in a bad state. Hopefully we're working on a package of money to be able to convert them into a launderette, and a store for nearly new clothing and refurbished furniture, which is what local people want. It isn't only just to get more resources for people, it will be used as an opportunity to get some training, to learn customer services type skills, or business management.'

The Furnival Newsletter for January 2000 tells us: 'March 31st should, we hope, see three retail outlets, adjacent to the Furnival, being released to Verdon Street Enterprises. This is a company limited by guarantee, with all its Directors being local people. It will provide a launderette, Advocacy Centre, CAB, Credit Union, nearly new clothes and refurbished furniture.'

Jane continued, 'We're getting into initiatives that the government are encouraging, like intermediate labour market jobs. Interestingly, the young girl who Josie managed to get back to court on Wednesday may be able to get a job here, learning some office skills, paid for by the government. We haven't got money but we'll fund-raise. And she will then be another sign of hope that will be a powerful picture for her family.

The Word made flesh

'Our society is not supporting people at the point of their need, we're rather saying, "Get your act together and come and join in the party." But Jesus says, "No, the feast is where you are." And people have got to discover that feast, which is why Josie is the key. We celebrate the writings of Paul in the Bible, but I want to celebrate the writings of Josie, not in words, but in her life of loving people into new ways of being. She's a 24-hour-a-day sermon. "Preach all day, but only use words when you have to", it's the Word made flesh, that stays flesh in Josie, whereas the clergy so often want to make the flesh into word again, and preach it, but stay at a safe distance. I think you've got to be lost in, hidden among, and then you'll see the resourcing of God in this place. If we get the package from the city, we'll have raised something like half a million pounds, and that's crazy! The resources of God are more than we can believe if we are in the flow of God's energy. But we try and trap God in church.

'I'm very passionate about not helping people to escape out of one scene just to be trapped into material things or into another scene. When Jesus took the child as the picture of the way to the Kingdom, he was giving us a very big challenge. We mustn't be reliant on ourselves, we mustn't be reliant on our wealth or our position, which is why women in more visibly impoverished parts of the world are doing fantastic things, because they're not blocking the energy of God working in them and among them to bring about change. I want people to find their freedom in the truth of the love of God – that sums me up. Nothing more, nothing less.'

THE CATHEDRAL CENTRE, SALFORD

In Salford we stayed with Kathleen King in her flat, a quiet haven which she returns to after busy days at the Cathedral's drop-in centre. Kathleen is a member of Pamela's congregation, the Society of the Holy Child Jesus, and she had arranged for us to visit the Centre, of which she was virtually the manager at the time, although she preferred to think of herself as one of the team.

Next morning Kathleen took us down to the basement next door to Salford Cathedral. The contrast between the mighty structure symbolizing the power and influence of the Church, and the lowly, hidden premises open to lowly, hidden people, is striking. Before our meeting with the volunteers, Kathleen told us about the people who come to the Centre, and their hopes or rather their lack of hope.

More than soup and blankets

'I think they come to the Centre primarily because once you're through the door, there are all the facilities. When they're living on the streets they can come here for a shower, they can change their clothes, get something to eat and sit around where it's warm and comfortable and safe. I think that's the first reason for coming. The great affirmation for me is seeing people gradually relax, come in and smile – a smile is one thing we try to give them when they come in.' As the Centre's Christmas 1999 letter put it, 'What they need is support and understanding, acceptance and love. The services we provide in the Centre – the hot food, showers, laundry, advice, clothing, etc., go some way to meet the need, but only if we offer them in such a way as to help build up a person's sense of dignity and self-worth and appropriate self-love. We always try to help people to move forward, for example in finding accommodation or seeking help for an addiction problem.'

The people using the Centre are very isolated individuals, who either have no relations or have lost touch with them. 'Making friends on the streets is impossible. They say to me, "You don't trust anybody", even people you kip with and share with, you don't trust them.

'What sends them out on the streets? The wife dying, the wife leaving, or putting them out for drink problems. A lot of it is alcohol related. And once you're on the streets you've got to keep drinking. It's almost impossible to stop once you're out. Most of the young ones are using drugs, but with the older men it's drink, and they look down on the drug users!

The crossword puzzle group

'But you do see people who always sit together. There's one group at the moment who do the crossword puzzle together every evening; the man who organizes it is more held together than the others, I don't know why he comes, but I think nobody comes without a reason. The group began as just friendship. A lot of people come in with mental illness, and the ones who sit with him have all got schizophrenia or something like that. They're all clever people, but the mental illness has hit them. One lad, for instance, he's about 23 now, has done his degree at Salford University. He's very sick, but he'll join in this group.'

We saw very few women the day we were there, perhaps two or three out of about 15 or 20 clients. 'I think that's mainly because most women have somewhere to be, and maybe children or grandchildren dependent on them, and so they can't come in. But the ones who do come in have all got big multiple problems. Why else would a woman come and sit in this heavy smoky atmosphere all day?'

But even in this apparently hopeless situation, hope was not entirely dead. Kathleen told us that most of them had hopes of coming out of it, though they needed a lot of support when they did. 'We've got individuals who've stopped drinking, have got flats, have got settled, even got jobs, and one still comes in virtually every day. I suppose our support is so important to them: it's so difficult to change your life if you've been a heavy drinker for years. You can't be friends with the people you've been drinking with, and who else do you make friends with? They seem to have no resources, nothing to fill their time.

'I don't believe in God'

'A lot of them have some kind of religious faith. For instance, this alcoholic had a woman friend who died recently. He was very, very cut up about it and was crying and telling me all about it, and then he said, "I don't believe in God at all", and after a bit, "I've had a Mass said for her." He tried his hardest to work round that! There's a funny side to it: he got her ashes back and asked the landlord at the pub she used to go to if he could sprinkle the ashes round where she sat. And the landlord said, "Well, yes, but I'll have to hoover them up in the morning!" He did it. He's still got a whole load more and he doesn't know where to put the rest.

The Jesus Army

'A lot of them get sucked up into the Jesus Army or these groups that go round the town at night, picking people up from the soup runs and places – they offer them accommodation and they help them, but they demand that they follow them and go to church. We had two men of very low intelligence who would come in and say, "We're preaching next week." You couldn't understand what Gordon was saying half the time, but they were being taken all round the country, and they were standing up and saying something.'

The tactics used by the sects, though open to criticism, at least give people a feeling of self-worth and a sense that they are contributing something to the community. Kathleen felt that the response of the Catholic Church was so inadequate. 'We haven't got that welcome, we haven't got that feeling of community in the church. We go in, we pray, and we walk out again. It's not Christianity, is it?'

In November 1999 Louise Casey, the government's so-called
'homelessness czar', in an article about rough sleepers, said that
although people were being helped to survive on the streets, with
the help of soup runs for instance, 'no one was helping them to
make any real difference to their lives. No one was helping them
to get their lives back together so they could come off the streets
permanently. [. . .] I do believe that some of the help given to
rough sleepers, however well-meaning, is misplaced.' These
remarks drew heavy criticism from the many organizations like the
Cathedral Centre that aim to build people up, as the Christmas
letter quoted above makes abundantly clear. Even in our short visit
we could see that those coming to the Centre, however odd they
may have looked and behaved, were treated gently and compas-
sionately, and thus were helped to cope with their lives.

After our conversation with Kathleen King, we met Clare
Edwards, Susan Morgan, Muriel Cordingley and Jane Kearsley,
four volunteer workers at the Centre. Marigold began by saying
something about the women we had met in El Salvador in 1994,
and how important it had been for us, and also for them, to listen
to their stories.

'Oh, there's a person here!'

Clare picked up the point about the importance of listening and
related it to her experience in the Centre. 'What you said about
people needing to have someone listen to them, and listen to what
happened to them, is like what happens here. That's what you find
quite a lot downstairs with the clients: they've had bad experiences
of life, and many of them, sooner or later, are glad to open up
about it. I think they benefit just from someone listening – not
necessarily being able to offer any solution, but listening with the
respect and concern which they don't get by and large from
people outside. I think we give them something different downstairs – it's not just a hand-out. We look at every person that comes
as a person of value, and that's the first response, "Oh, there's a
person here!" Before I came here and had only seen them outside,
some of them looked so weird and I'd think, "Gosh, I'd rather
keep away from that." But you don't see them anonymously like

that, you see them as people; you hope to give a personal response, first of all as a person with a life and a story, and troubles or pleasures. The food is incidental. It's just part of that respect and that concern – like you invite people into your home for a meal, and that's an acknowledgement of their importance to you.'

Sue added, 'You can never judge a book by its cover. Downstairs we have people of supreme intelligence, giftedness, abilities of every kind, which are unknown unless you sit down and listen to them. We have a lot of addiction problems; people say, "I don't like myself", so we're the first in the line of listening to somebody and getting to the point where you can help them to see themselves more positively.'

We went downstairs for lunch in the Centre and sat at a table with three men who were 'old hands', and three newcomers to the Centre. We had a good talk with them and appreciated what Sue had said about not judging a book by its cover. We realized that both a scruffy exterior, and indeed a well-groomed exterior, like that of the woman client we spoke with later, can conceal great potential as well as a tragic life story.

More hope in El Salvador?

Clare remarked that the people in El Salvador seemed to have a great sense of self-worth and of their own dignity, whereas many of the people who come to the Centre feel they are failures. They feel judged by our very materialistic society, by those materialistic expectations, and they see no hope for themselves. 'So there is at the heart of a lot of them a deep sense of despair and hopelessness, which comes out in various ways, addiction, or violence, or drugs, or alcohol. It's very difficult in our type of society to see any way in which they can climb out. Funnily enough, there seems to be more hope for those at the bottom in El Salvador than there is here.'

Jane told us about Joanne, an alcoholic in a violent relationship. 'She took terrible, terrible beatings, she was so low. Then one day, I don't know where she found the strength, she left him. She's still an alcoholic, but the wicked beatings are over. I think she's getting her self-esteem back again. We've been saying to her, "You're worth more than this", and one day she came and said she'd done it.'

Sue thought our society was very judgemental about women. 'I remember when everything came out about Mary Bell, she looked to her childhood, and she said, "It doesn't provide an excuse for what I did, but it does provide an explanation." And I think we get to the point downstairs where people tell us about their childhood, what happened to them, and the dreadful experiences they've endured, and that gives us the explanation for the person we see in front of us. But society doesn't see that, doesn't understand that.'

Muriel had found it difficult at first not to be judgemental. 'You have a conflict within yourself, you think, "What are these people doing here? Why can't they do something?" That's something I've had to try and work out, try to accept people as they are. Coming here and meeting the volunteers has been a tremendous strength. Their commitment and their relationship with the people – it's been a learning experience and a great privilege.'

Jane spoke about the shock she had when she went downstairs for the first time. 'It was like another world.' We then asked 'Which is the real world, the one we're in or the one they're in? You are facing the realities downstairs.'

'That's what I felt, all the time,' Clare said. 'As Jane said, it's the shock, and then you go home and you're in this relatively comfortable lifestyle where people have no idea. This is what life is really about, it's absolutely basic. I'm full of admiration for the clients, they just keep on and they keep at it. They might appear to be giving up, but they're still trying, in an obscure way. I think I get from them far more than I give.'

Sue agreed. 'That was my question in the beginning, who is caring for whom? We also have needs to be cared for and we also are vulnerable.'

Relationships with God

Clare remembered a conversation she had with a prostitute. 'She was in her middle years and she was as lively and as natural as could be, apparently. Then she got talking and it became very clear that right down at the bottom there was a real anguish because she'd lost her children and had no contact with them except from a distance. She felt she'd blown everything, she couldn't do anything except exist from day to day. But she said what a lot of them do in the end, she said her prayers. They have new relationships with God almost as if that's the only lifeline. People have let them down all the time, and people will carry on letting them down, there's no faith in people, but maybe there's someone up there who in some obscure way will look after them in the end, or look after their children.'

Sadly, their experience of church was negative. They didn't come up to society's expectations, neither did they come up to the Church's expectations. Clare asked, 'But is it a Christian ideal the Church is holding up? I think it's a false ideal. It's not true of Christianity. It should be love and growth and openness and cherishing, and what they're getting is violence and rejection, and condemnation.'

ANAWIM, BALSALL HEATH – MAKING FRIENDS ON THE STREET

ANAWIM, Women Working Together, is a project offering friendship, hospitality, support and a way out to women involved in prostitution. As their leaflet says, 'The project operates on the basic belief in the worth, dignity, and the innate goodness of each individual – and a belief in the positive potential of each individual for growth, change and development.'

Our visit was arranged by Catriona McPhail, a Holy Child sister like Pamela, and we met with her and Sister Enda Gorman (Our Lady of Charity) in a small ground-floor room in the cramped terrace house, which buzzed with life. The project for helping prostitutes had grown out of the work of two sisters of Our Lady of Charity, Magdalene and Maisie, who came to work in Balsall Heath in 1986 with a rehabilitation project for drug addicts and alcoholics, run by Father Hudson's Society.

Reaching out

Enda joined Magdalene and Maisie in 1992, 'when we really started working full time in relation to women. From then on we went out on the street three nights a week and met different women. We felt we were meeting a good number of women who wanted to talk a bit more, but didn't have time on the streets, so we decided we would open the house on a Thursday evening and welcome the women in. We see ourselves as befriending women, and that means building up a relationship, anywhere, be it hospital, prison, whatever, to be there for them.' From the outreach work, and the Centre in Mary Street, the work developed to include a safe house, Sarabeth (to give the women the time, space and support they need to look at any changes they want to make in their lives), and the Women's Development Project, offering training in a variety of skills (with a crèche and trained worker). Catriona was manager of the development project.

The volunteers are an indispensable element in keeping all this going: some work in the house, some visit the women in their homes, some study the legalization issues, others are involved in awareness-raising, speaking to groups about the effects of prostitution on women. 'No woman', said Enda, 'is in prostitution voluntarily. People have a thing about prostitution, thinking that women enjoy it and really get a kick out of it. But it's quite the opposite, women are very oppressed in prostitution, they suffer from the pimp, they suffer from the punters, they suffer from the neighbourhood they live in, they suffer through the courts, through the police very often – they are in a very precarious position. Violence all round.'

The Wednesday group

This had begun as a coffee morning, with six or seven women, giving them an opportunity to meet and support each other, 'And it has proved invaluable. They have gained a tremendous amount from the friendship. Life is very isolating for a woman in this work, they don't have friends on the streets because they are all vying for the same customers, and the pimps don't encourage women to make friendships with one another.'

Julie, one of the ex-prostitutes, later told us, 'The Wednesday group's strong because everyone is coming out with the same thing, you can understand each other. It's hard for a person who has never done anything to understand what we went through. To be understood and not judged.'

Maria, when Pamela called her a tough woman, said, 'I'm learning to be tough. I never used to be. Coming to the Wednesday group, it's given me so much courage to speak about things.'

Four brave women

Clare, Jayne, Julie and Maria then arrived with their children, who were settled in the next room with Janine, the childcare worker, and after coffee and biscuits they began telling us the sad stories of their lives, which had been ruled for so long by pimps and violence. All were now out of prostitution.

Clare's story

A television programme had told the story of Lucy, a 17-year-old prostitute in Walsall, who had been picked up, taken to a flat, given pure heroin, and died. Clare said, 'That's what got me off the streets, watching that. Seeing the danger. I mean, actually experiencing the danger was different, it's part of everyday life, but when you're sat watching the programme, I thought, "I've got to stop this, or I'm going to be the next one that's going to be found dead." When I was down there on the streets obviously I was drinking and taking drugs, I didn't see the danger. I experienced it, but I didn't see it. But when I saw that – everyone slagged it down so much, but it was so close to reality, and I saw the way families were affected in the programme. My mum said she felt like that, every time she knew I was going on the streets she wondered whether a policeman was going to knock on the door to say, "We found your daughter's body." That was it, I felt I couldn't stand that. My mum had a lot better understanding when she'd seen the programme from what she'd heard from me. She'd heard the glamour side, "I'm getting loads of money, I'm buying new clothes", but she saw the reality then and she understood it a little bit better. And my Nan.

It's always there

'When I was asked to go on television to talk about my story, my mum said, "But Clare, you finished with prostitution two years ago, why can't you just leave it all behind?" And I said, "Because it won't let me, it's always there." It's a part of your life that's always going to be there. Now I've had that experience, it's like a big desire within me to help other women, it's like I know what a prostitute goes through, and if I can help them, I will. The thing that upsets me most is this thing about the record – it's going to be on my record for the rest of my life, and I never knew that until after I'd finished.' (This, of course, makes it very difficult to get an ordinary job. 'Sorry, you're not suitable', they are told.)

Clare had never had a pimp. 'I already distrusted men anyway, so I knew not to trust anyone. So I didn't allow it to happen.' Pamela asked if that didn't put her in more danger and Clare replied, 'Oh yes, a lot more. I got raped three times.'

Julie added, 'Even if you're working for someone, you still don't get protection anyway, so the danger's the same whether you're working for someone or not. They're just there to get the money out of you.'

An important seminar

A few weeks previously the women had attended a seminar run by the organization WAITS (Women Active In Today's Society). This group was aware of the difficulties for women who wanted to leave prostitution. The seminar gave them the opportunity to speak of what they had experienced, the obstacles that were there and the lack of resources. Julie broke with prostitution many years ago, Clare is three years out of prostitution. Julie's comment on the seminar was, 'Lots of those things that were haunting me went away.'

Maria's story

'I actually convicted my pimp,' she told us. When she was 16, her boyfriend's brothers kidnapped her from a nightclub and took her to London and put her on the street. 'He followed me. I worked in London for about a year. Then the beatings just got so bad and there wasn't enough money left. I confided in a police officer, he actually saw what was happening and he went out of his way to arrest me. He helped me get away. I lived under police protection for two years while the trial was being settled. My pimp found me, I got beat up again and left for dead, and it went to court and he got two years and was out in 18 months.'

Maria said the police had done everything possible to help her and to get this man convicted and the result was a sentence that he just laughed at as he was sent down. Maria's conclusion was, 'I would never do it again. If I had the choice of saying, "Do I send him to court, do I get him locked up, or do I just let it go?", I'd just let it go. It's more trouble than it's worth. All this pain, all this running away.

'He defended himself in court, he questioned me. It shouldn't be allowed because the sorts of question he was throwing at me, there was so much fear inside of me – how do I answer this question? If I don't answer it right he could walk away, if I do answer it right, when he comes out what's he going to do to me? It shouldn't be allowed to happen.' (The recent Youth Justice and Criminal Evidence Act removed the right of defendants to cross-examine complainants themselves.)

You can run but you can never hide

'The day I had him locked up he says to me, "You can run but you can never hide", and his brother came round and says to me, "It might be five years, or ten, or twenty, but he will make you pay." And I believe it. I'm still looking over my shoulder and I will be for the rest of my life. I don't think at this moment he knows where I am, but I think if he really wanted to find me he would. He did it before – I was living in Bournemouth and he found me. I just got to the stage where I'm not running away no more. Birmingham is my home, I'm staying put. I've got two children, the eldest lives with my mum and dad. I'm just going to get on with my life, and when it happens it happens.'

Jayne's story

'I used to ask the police to arrest me so they could keep me in longer, because after you've been in, you get the charge sheet, and when you're released your pimp can see when you were picked up and when you were released, so he can't actually beat you if you've been picked up. But then he used to say, "Well, it's your own fault for getting picked up, you shouldn't have been there." You cannot, you cannot, win.'

Jayne had got out of prostitution because when she was six months pregnant her pimp had kicked her. 'For a few weeks I was all right, then I lost the baby. There was no evidence to say the kicking had caused it, because it was a few weeks later, but I think it was. I think he'd done some damage somewhere. But of course I went back again after, then he wanted me back on the street, and I said, "No". I did go back on the street for a while. When I was pregnant with Nicola I just walked away from him altogether. I thought, "He's not going to get a chance to do it again. There's no way." Ten years ago I stopped doing prostitution but he wanted me to go back. He kept saying, "We can leave", but we never did leave. "We can have this, we can have that." It was always him that had things, not me. I never had anything. They say "I love you, I'll do anything for you." So you say, "Well, I'll stop doing it then." He says 'Oh, well, no, you're used to doing it now." You're used to it, and what does it matter, you know? Once I had a mark round my neck from some man trying to strangle me. I was passing out, and he said, "Well, you're all right, you're still alive, what are you complaining about?" I could have been dead. And that's when you know they don't give a damn about you. I could have been lying dead somewhere.'

'And then,' said Clare, 'you've got to go home and have sex with him at the end of the night . . .'

'No,' interrupted Julie, 'you don't have sex with him . . .'

'You're making love, yeah!' responded Clare, to general laughter.

'It's all about power, isn't it?'

That was Clare's verdict, when the women were talking about whether to stand up to a violent pimp or just take it. They agreed that standing up to him often made the violence worse whereas if you were submissive it was over quicker. Julie commented, 'If you don't cry then you're trying to be brave or strong – you can take it. You need to be that weak person that they want, so if you just cry, a couple of slaps . . . But sometimes you can cry and because you're crying they want to do more, for you to cry more. You can't win.'

The children

The women spoke to us for an hour and a half; their openness was a tribute to the ANAWIM community – they obviously felt that anyone ANAWIM invited was worthy of their trust. We ended by inviting the children to join their mothers, learning their names, and taking a photograph.

An inner strength

We did not feel it was appropriate to ask whether some kind of religious faith had any part in their lives – the fact that they had survived horrendous experiences, and had come through smiling and determined to make something of their lives spoke to us of an inner strength, and of a desire to respond to the faith that the ANAWIM community had clearly invested in them.

The new ANAWIM

Some time later we visited ANAWIM again in their new, roomy premises. It was good to see Julie and Jayne again and we also talked with Catriona McPhail's successor as manager of the Women's Development Programme, Frances Hefter, who updated us:

'We're now doing outreach two nights in the week, one couple will go from 10 to 12pm, and the other team will go

12 to 2am. We've been meeting between ten and 15 women within two hours. We always take out coffee, tea, drinking chocolate, biscuits, and we invite the women to come and sit in the car if they'd like to, and have a drink and a chat. All of them have difficult stories, so we let them talk and get rid of some of that burden. Then we will offer to meet them and talk at other times, or we give them our card with the number on, so they can ring up or come to the Centre. Very few of the women we meet then actually avail themselves of the offer, but we have given them the opportunity, they know there's a door there. We now meet for a full day on Wednesday, and also on Tuesday.'

'We've seen women blossoming . . .'

Frances told us, 'And it's very good to see that. The programme makes the women feel accepted for who they are, as women, rather than being labelled as prostitutes. It has to be their decision to come out of prostitution, nobody can make them do anything, it doesn't work that way. But through working with them, talking with them, accepting them, they can gradually move forward. Sometimes they slip back, and that's really hard. But at the end of the day, if they've had the experience of being here, meeting people, and just the friendly atmosphere, that doesn't go away. It does help them just meeting other women who are out of prostitution. Any woman is accepted back unconditionally.'

The Women's Development Project helps the women build up their abilities and skills, once they have regained their self-confidence and feeling of self-worth. There had been a lot of babies that year, so the women hadn't been doing other things, 'But now there's much more of a movement towards wanting to do things, so we do various crafts, like glass painting and sewing. One woman is excellent on the sewing machine, she made a lot of things. It's really good to see them learning these skills and blossoming.' There were sometimes obstacles in the way of women going to an outside class. 'One was going to an outside college, but the fellow she is with is too possessive, and oppressive, and has whisked her away. There's a lot of possessiveness, violence and oppression, and there's the drug scene as well. We help the women to access de-tox programmes.'

A happy respite

The activities include holidays, parties and barbecues in the summer. Generous benefactors offered holiday houses free of charge, so that the women and their children were able to get away for a time. Frances described a recent holiday, which had been hugely successful. 'There were a lot of different experiences for them, it wasn't the sort of holiday they'd had before. I've found quite a change since then, it's been a very good experience. I found it very beneficial getting to know the women more on that level, and some of the children as well. You get to know people much better when you're living with them 24 hours a day. We took eight women, 13 children, and babies. The women loved it, I don't think I've heard any adverse comments at all. Someone said, "It was really good to be able to get away completely from the drug scene." It's so difficult in a city like this, where there are drugs everywhere, and particularly in an area like this where the women live.'

Nothing for tea

Marigold remarked that it must be a terrible temptation, when the financial situation gets really bad, to slip back into prostitution. Frances agreed, 'Well, that's the thing – getting things for the children, or a big bill comes in, and that's the way they know to make money. We do find the women going out towards Christmas, because they want to buy everything that's on the television, and the children want what's on the television. But sometimes we've met women on the streets who have said, "Well, there was nothing in the cupboard. There was nothing for tea, so I had to go out and get some money, to get something for the kids' tea."'

So easy to get into, so hard to get out

During our earlier meeting with the four women they explained how easy it is to get trapped in prostitution, even addicted to it. 'It's so easy to get into,' said Clare.

'Especially when you've got no money', added Jayne. 'You want to stop but you don't stop. Not overnight anyway.' Catriona stressed how difficult it is just to walk away from a violent pimp, especially if you've got children.

'You do walk away in the end', concluded Jayne, 'but you've got to have had enough of it first, and it might take some longer than others. When you're ready to go off you will.'

Clare told us that it had taken her mother ten years to walk out on her abusive stepfather. 'Alcohol had been her only way of getting away from the pain of all the bad beatings, the emotional abuse and the rape. Finally they copped him and that was it. She'd had enough. I look at my mum now and I can't believe she's pulled through, that she's still there and still standing up for her family.'

Out of sight, out of mind

Balsall Heath is a largely Asian neighbourhood. In 1995 a vigilante system was set up, mainly by Asian men, to clear the streets of prostitutes. 'Two-faced', Clare called them.

'They go driving around for the women', said Julie, 'then all of a sudden they turn and want to get them off their streets.'

'They don't want their children seeing us', Jayne thought.

Clare remembered standing out there at the time. 'There was about 30 men and ten women vigilantes and they just harassed us and paraded around us all the time. They kidnapped a few of the girls.'

Eventually, Catriona told us, they started to harass any single woman walking along the streets. So now the public might think there is no prostitution in Balsall Heath but the women said it's just moved to somewhere else, or into flats, which is much more dangerous for the women as they are out of reach of help. Or else, said Clare, they come out on the streets at 2am when the vigilantes are not around, 'And that is the most dangerous time, because you've got all the weirdos driving around.'

'And all the restaurant bosses coming out of the restaurants', added Jayne. 'They're all Asian fellers. They're the ones that drive around at that time in the morning.'

Behind closed doors

'If you do it in a house, on your own, that's all right,' explained Clare. 'They can't prove it if it's just you behind closed doors, but when you're coming back and forth with different men it's classed as a business establishment.' Brothels these days disguise themselves as saunas.

'Advertised as No Prostitution', said Jayne. 'They can't have a man running it, because he mustn't live off immoral earnings. They always have a woman that hasn't got a criminal record.'

'The madam,' said Clare. 'There was one on TV the other night and she kept going on about how it's not immoral, it doesn't affect their lives afterwards, it's such a wonderful profession. There were three other women there – admittedly they were doing it the right way, getting £1,000 a week.'

'They stop you if you're doing it for a fiver,' added Julie.

Clare insisted that even if those women were doing it from choice, 'They're still victims, and they'll realize it when they stop'.

Clare, Jayne, Julie and Maria were adamant that they had never had a real choice. 'You're going to get a beating if you don't go out, so you go out.'

We went away full of admiration for them all and for their good friends at ANAWIM.

THE CEDARWOOD TRUST, WOMEN'S WRITING GROUP

At the invitation of Jo Forster, whom we had met on our first visit to Newcastle, we went up to the North East again a few months later, and stayed with Jo and her husband John in Whitley Bay. On our first morning David Peel, an Anglican priest, picked us up and took us to the Cedarwood Trust on the Meadow Well Estate in North Shields. David, who is project leader, and Sheila Auld, another Anglican priest, are two of the team of five project workers.

The Meadow Well Estate

Built in the 1930s to clear the Bankside slums from the edge of the River Tyne, the estate very soon became overcrowded. Even after it was redone in the 60s, it was filled up with people who had nowhere else to go or who had terrible problems. An article in *The Independent Magazine*, January 1991, commented: 'Jobs [. . .] have been disappearing inexorably over the years, with nothing to replace them, to the extent that these days 96 per cent of people on the Meadowell [sic] are receiving some form of state benefit. [. . .] Virtually no one leaves the estate to go to work, so virtually no one leaves the estate.'

When Sheila Auld came to Cedarwood in 1988 it was on South Meadow Well, four terraced houses knocked into one, with rooms for community use downstairs, furnished with a washing machine and dryer, where people could come for a cup of tea and a chat. When the estate was redeveloped, they moved into the tiny flat where we met, but Sheila told us they were hoping, if they got Lottery funding, to expand, have a proper children's room and an art room, and more staff. (Since our visit this hope has been fulfilled.)

The Writing Group

The Meadow Well Centre is open for the use of different groups from Monday to Friday, 9.30am to 1pm. The Cedarwood Women's Writing Group, led by Sheila, meets every week. When we arrived they were laying out a bring-and-share lunch. The group round the table – Elaine, Angela, Jean, Ellen, Linda, Pat, and Diane – didn't need any persuasion, but began talking and telling their stories, sometimes all at once! Linda and Elaine were eloquent in their praise of Cedarwood and of the support the workers gave them. Both of them had had problems with their children, and as Linda said, 'Sheila helped me with those problems. Sheila and David don't just stop at home and wait for you to come and talk to them, they come out and talk to you and help you with all sorts of different problems. It's a big help getting everything off your chest, and also writing things down.' Elaine came to the Centre three times a week. 'I couldn't cope without Sheila and David. If I didn't have them to talk to, I wouldn't have anybody. I've just been grateful that they've been there. I've never shown me feelings before, I've never let anyone know I've been upset. But I just couldn't keep it in any longer and Sheila has helped a lot.'

Jean was a heavy smoker and had recently been confined to the house for four days with a bad cough, on her own most of the time. 'Nobody to talk to, nobody came when you needed them. You canna ring up and say, "I'm not well, come round", can you?' Chorus: 'Yes, you can!' Her experience of loneliness at this time made her feel for others in the same situation, and Marigold commented, 'But that's lovely, to turn your own difficulty and pain into wanting to help other people in their situation.'

As with the other centres we visited, it was the companionship that was appreciated above all, the being able to share one's story with others, to know one was not alone. In these places listening has been elevated to a fine art!

Another very important aspect of this ministry is the giving and nurturing of a sense of dignity and self-worth by encouraging people to do things they didn't think they had it in them to do, broadening experiences, showing them that there is something else in life, making them feel worth something. For instance, last year Sheila obtained funding from the Lottery, through the Arts Council, to enable 16 of the women to take part in a series of weekends away in Northumberland. While there they wrote and recorded a radio play, 'Seven for a Secret'. The main character, Melissa, was pregnant and she recited a poem 'Let Me Out', which was about a baby due to be born. This poem, with others, was published in *Shared Feelings, Mixed Emotions*, the group's second book. The first book, *Mixed Feelings*, was used by Amber Films of Newcastle to make the film 'Dream On'. The principle behind the writing is, as Sheila said, 'Writing it down helps you to cope.'

The women had contributed to a variety of other events, ranging from the Archbishop of Canterbury's Garden Party at Lambeth Palace, to the local Metrocentre, thronged with shoppers, where they performed in the main shopping area, and including a service in St Gabriel's, Heaton, Sheila's church.

Shared problems

The women were touched by the photographs of the Salvadorean women that we showed them, and their stories. They felt that they shared some of the same problems, especially male domination, and violence.

One of the women told a story of the violence she had suffered from her husband, which was horrific. 'This night he came in he'd been drinking. It was Good Friday, I'll never forget it.' He took a black marker and marked out on her body how he was going to cut her up. He went upstairs and brought down some cases which he lined with black bin bags so no one would see he was carrying her body. 'He had it all planned. I went upstairs, he had a big knife, he'd sharpened it and everything, he had the steel on the bed where he'd been sharpening the knife, all the bed was lined with bin bags. The next thing was I had a knife in me hand, I stabbed him in the arm and managed to get out of the house to me friend's house. I got fined for it, for stabbing him. The best £15 I've ever spent in me life! At first they had me for attempted murder, then they said it was manslaughter, but because he was still alive and because of the background that I had, it came down to the fine. The court gave him my house and I had to go and live with me mum and dad with the kids. People say, "Well, why do you stay with a man like that?" It makes me really angry. It really bugs me. They just don't understand. Where are you to go?'

The two lines at the end of *Shared Feelings, Mixed Emotions* are a fitting epilogue to the experiences of these women:

> Keep up the good work, continue your writing
> and as you said, sharing is a new way of fighting.

Sheila's story

'When I came here it was almost a coincidence – if you can call these things coincidences! I went to Shepherds Dean retreat house to join in discussion about setting up the Church Urban Fund, and David happened to be there with some people from Cedarwood. It was the first time I'd heard of Meadow Well, but after several other coincidences I got the job here. After I'd been working at Cedarwood for a while, David had to leave and worked elsewhere for just over two years. Another David [Herbert] took his place. When, after two years, *he* decided to leave he suggested that I take on the job as project leader. I said, "Oh no, I couldn't do that, I can't sit at the desk all day, I want to be among the people. And anyway they always like someone who is ordained to be the project leader." And David said, "Wonderful idea! Why don't you get ordained?" It had never entered my head before then. I told various people and they said, 'Wonderful idea, Sheila! Go and talk to the vicar." So I did and I suddenly found I was ordained! That was four years ago.

'It is wonderful. I remember the principal of the course saying, 'You know, you'll be treated very differently when you're ordained", and I said, "I won't, because those people know me so well. They're not going to change." And they haven't. They always seem very proud of me. They all came to my ordination, and the first time I presided at Holy Communion it was at the Community Centre down the road. There were people from my church there, and people from other churches round here, my family was there, and many people from Meadow Well were there. It was a lovely occasion. When I was lined up ready to go in, in all my robes, the caretaker of the place was standing at the door. We were all in procession, and the music started, and he said, "Break a leg, Sheila!"

The blessing through the bar pumps

'When I was giving out Communion I got a message from five ladies who had set up the tea cups and things in a bar at the back, they couldn't get out and come round, because they were blocked off, so they sent a message to say, "Will you please come and give us a blessing." So I had to lean through the bar pumps and give them a blessing! And I thought, "This is how it should be." The women are marvellous, they protect me as much as I look after them. If I go anywhere and they think some man is looking at me, they say, "Be careful of him, Sheila!", and they stand really close to me. We're like a family really. I'm very close to a lot of the women.

The men's group

'I work mainly with women and children under five, but a lot of the men come here in the mornings to talk, and a lot of people with mental health problems who are on medication and have nowhere else to go. At the moment we have more men than women. We don't ask for a reason for coming in, you can just come in and talk and be yourself. David is trying to get a men's group started. It's quite difficult for the men on this estate because they've lost so much. They haven't got jobs, most of them are unemployed. All the ship-building's gone, the mining's gone, the fishing industry's gone right down, and there's nothing to take their place, so some of the men have become very silent, they don't know what to do with themselves.

'The women are the ones who've got to get the children to school, they're the strong ones in this way. They make the effort to get these awful jobs where they're not paid very much, cleaning jobs and care jobs; some of them go down to the quayside and take the tails off prawns, they spend all night doing this terrible job for hardly any pay. They have such troubled lives.

The fear of new places

'Their roots are here. Some of them hardly move off this estate. One of the difficulties we have if we want to take people away, is the fear of new places. I do a trip to Iona every year with about ten adults. Some of them drop out the week before we are due to go because they just can't make that step. But others after two days there say, "I don't want to go home, I want to live here. I want everyone to come and live here with us. Aren't the people wonderful?" They make friends with people, have their addresses and write to them when they get home. Iona is one of the nicest places because they don't ask any questions, everybody's welcome to the services. The people I take go in and stand among the others there, and when the Communion comes round they take a piece of bread and have a sip of wine. I think it's just how it should be. They love the singing and they've taken part in bits of the service, reading or joining in the prayers. And afterwards they have said, "I really enjoyed that!"

'It was different for me'

'I was divorced and left on my own with four children, I lived on benefits for ages. Then I remarried, and my husband died after 16 months, but he happened to die somewhere where no one could find him, so I was searching for him for three years. I was hard up, I remember my son putting plastic bags in his shoes because he wanted to go on a hike. But I had people round me who weren't in the same state. People from church came and emptied their cupboards for me when I was first on my own, and the second time too. And the church gave me £20 to get me by. People around would never have let me go under. If I had a bill that was difficult to pay, someone would find out and pay it for me. People here often say, "Well, you were in that situation, weren't you, Sheila, so what did you do?" So I can say, "Well, this is what I did." But actually it's not the same. It was awful but it's not the same as them. They don't have the same support and they don't have a strong faith. My church is very supportive of them because I preach about them, I say "There's a woman in this difficult situation", and they come and offer to help. But they can't get help like that for themselves, because everyone round them is in the same situation. They're brave, they're very brave people. A young woman sits there every week and chats and laughs, and yet her life is so hard. She's got hardly any money, and her house is not decorated, and you think, "How do they get themselves out of it?"

A kind of faith

'Lots of them when I first got ordained wanted their children baptized, so we had a joint ecumenical baptism and that was really memorable. I don't know whether for them it was tradition or superstition, but at the same time, a lot of them do have a kind of faith, and that's the faith you have to get hold of and encourage and go along with. You know there's something there, and I think sometimes they don't realize what it is. Once we went to Fingal's Cave from Iona, and we went up on the cliffs, and all the puffins came and sat round us. Well, one woman is very keen on wild life and she absolutely loved the puffins – the sun was shining and it was just beautiful. She got back in the boat – she is not someone who's demonstrative because of her difficult past – and she said to me, "I know you'll think this silly, Sheila, but I want to give you a great big kiss." And I thought, "Well, I know that God is doing this." And she was so happy and lifted up, and I thought, "Well, that's when I recognize that God is here, and whether *they* know it or not, I know." And then you talk about it, and they sometimes say, "Why did I feel like that?"

'They feel alienated going to a church, they feel they shouldn't be there, but when they came and took part in a service at my church they said, "Oh, if your church was near we'd come all the time, Sheila." I don't suppose they would, but it is a lovely bright, friendly church. We're hoping, when we get the space downstairs, that we'll have a quiet room. We had one in the other Centre. We'd say, 'We're just going up to pray, do you want to come?" And one or two of them would say, "Yes, I'll come." And if someone said, "Would you say a prayer for my Bobby, Sheila?" it was something. I think it would be much better if we had something like that to offer them than trying anything else, really. It's difficult, though.'

❧ 5 ❧

A Place of Refuge

We had been distressed that so many of the women we talked with had experienced violence from their partners, so we were particularly interested and encouraged to hear about the work being done to help women and children who have fled their homes and found refuge with OWA. There was so much to learn that we had three separate meetings to hear about different aspects of the work from different members of staff.

First of all a project worker in charge of one of the safe houses came and met with us at Marigold's house. (Naturally OWA is extremely careful to keep the addresses of the safe houses secret.) She told us that Women's Aid is a national organization which was started by women for women in the 1970s. Oxfordshire Women's Aid was set up in 1975 as an independent, registered charity and now has three houses in Oxford city centre. Part of the project worker's job is staffing the OWA advice line which is open Monday to Friday 9.30–5.00. 'It gives telephone support to women if they want to talk about what is happening at home, about legal problems, telephoning their solicitors, what their rights are, or if they just want to talk about how they're feeling. We have referrals coming from other refuges which ask us if we have space for a woman if it's not safe to stay where she is, and we have referrals from health visitors, from doctors, from social workers who want advice about how to tackle a problem, or what a woman does if she has to leave her home at once.

A safe place to go

'We have to manage the houses, so when a woman comes into my house I'm her key worker from the minute she arrives. I settle her into her bedroom and deal with any problems she might have, such as where to go to get her benefit or where the nearest doctor's surgery is. Or she may just want to talk about what's been happening, how she's feeling. My job also is very practical. We have to maintain houses, deal with any repairs needed. If a woman comes in the middle of the night I have to see that the bed's been changed, the bedside light works, that kind of thing, a little bit like working in a hotel, not quite, though. We've got three houses. There are 13 bedrooms of different sizes, some for single women, some with bunk beds and a cot, so we could have a woman with a five-year-old and a baby, and we've got big family rooms with two lots of bunk beds and a cot. We could give a woman two adjacent rooms, so we could take someone with five or six children if need be.

'Sometimes there's a bit of conflict between women who haven't got children and those who have living in a shared house. They have their own room and their own food but they have to share a bathroom, a living room and a kitchen, so sometimes that can lead to problems. They make their own meals. They have their own food cupboards and perhaps one shelf in the fridge and one shelf in the freezer. There's a playroom in each of the houses for the children and we have a project manager and two project workers whose key responsibility is the children.'

They stress that they are not social workers. OWA is an independent charity which gets money from the local authority, the council, and from social services and charitable donations. But they do have responsibility for the women and for child protection. They have to make sure the houses meet the regulations for things like fire doors and the premises are inspected.

Encouraging independence

The staff don't live on the premises, we were told. 'We work from half-past nine until five. We have a main office in one of the houses where we do all the administration work and statistics. I manage one house, someone else manages another and we share the main house where the office is. We come in first thing in the morning, have an hour there to see what's happened during the night, then go over to our houses and clean up for a couple of hours, so we're only actually in the houses for about two hours a day. We work very much on an empowerment basis. When a woman first arrives she's in quite a state because she's got a lot on her mind but then after a couple of weeks we encourage her to make phone calls herself, to go to appointments on her own. If a woman's not feeling up to it, we will take her to the doctor or to the benefits office, but we try to orientate her so she can do things herself. We try and encourage her to be independent.

'After 5 o'clock we have an on-call system. There are five workers and we're each on-call for a week in turn, so if there's an emergency in any of the houses the women can page us and then we'll ring them at their house and see what's happening, and if necessary we can go to the house – like, last night we had a fire there! It was only a little kitchen fire, but that's the kind of thing. Or if a child is ill we can get them to a doctor.'

What if he finds her?

We asked what happens if an abusive partner finds out where the woman is. 'We haven't had anyone track a woman down yet. If a man does find out where the woman is, it's usually because the woman telephones him. The men manipulate the women. They'll say, "I'm going to hang myself, I'm going to commit suicide if you don't let me see you", trying to get the woman to tell him where she is. If he does find out where she is, we'll arrange for her to go to another refuge. You get these images of a man battering on the door, but that hasn't happened since I've been there. Really the women are quite safe once they get there. There are big reinforced doors with double locks and they've got spy-holes. But we recommend that the local women don't stay in Oxford, because as they go around they might be spotted either by their partner or his friends. We send them to places outside. The women here come from Manchester, Birmingham – all over. There is a referral system through the Samaritans or through the local police so the local refuge will ring round and try us, or vice versa. There's a whole network of refuges across the country, in most of the major towns.'

Cut off from family and friends

It was explained that a refuge is the last resort for women who can't afford to move into alternative accommodation and haven't got family to stay with. Often the mental cruelty they have been subjected to involves the man alienating the woman from her family and friends. 'When a woman talks to her sister the man will say, "Why are you talking to her? She doesn't like you. She's told me that she hates you." If she goes to visit family or friends, he says, "Where are you going? I don't want you to go there. I saw you talking to her in the street, I don't want you doing that." And in the end he'll totally isolate her, so if she does try and leave she's got nobody, all her friends have gone, all her family say, "You haven't phoned me for two years" and again that's a way of controlling her. It reduces her confidence to such a low level that trying to pick herself up is very difficult. And if every day you're waking up and the man is saying that you're ugly, you start to believe it, or if she's fat. One woman was huge and she went to Weightwatchers and she lost lots of weight and her husband just didn't know what to say to her. He said, "Oh you've done it for another man. You're having an affair. All the men are looking at you in the pub." It's jealousy – he's got to be in control of the woman and by her losing weight she's saying, "You're not going to control me any more, I'm going to do this for me." And I think that gave her a lot of strength.'

We learned that women stay in abusive relationships for many reasons: for the sake of the children (not realizing that staying can do the children more harm than leaving); because they don't think they can cope on their own; or because they still have feelings for their partner. The project worker described talking to women in the refuge and realizing they are missing their partners, though they don't want to admit it. 'They miss having a boyfriend, having someone lying next to them in bed. When they're upset they miss that kind of thing, though they don't miss the beatings. And of course some of the women have been abused as children and they crave love and they'll put up with anything if they think that their partner loves them, gives them the love they didn't have as a child.

We take her at her word

'A lot of the advice we give is meant to reinforce that it's not the woman's fault, it wasn't that she was doing something wrong. It's really important to get that message over. And that abuse is a crime, a charge can be brought and she'll be listened to. At Women's Aid we take a woman at her word. If she tells us on the phone that she is suffering domestic violence then we will accept that. We won't say, "Oh I'd better ring the police and double-check that." If she says she is, we accept that. Other agencies have to have proof, have to have the doctor's note, it has to be stated that she came in with a bruise or a fracture, but we don't do that. Just to be listened to, to know that someone is there who will listen and believe this is happening to them, does a lot for the women.'

They write poetry

We were given copies of a number of poems written by women in the refuge. We were told that some women who come in have already written quite a lot of poetry but for many it is a new way of expressing their feelings and trying to make sense of their experiences.

'What we tend to do, especially for the nights and the times when we're not there, we suggest it to them as an outlet, to get things down on paper, to try and work out what's going on in their minds. I personally would like to develop things like counselling or groups when the women can share their experiences. A lot of the women that come in do need counselling, and they need it *now*, but a lot of the counselling services have six-month waiting lists. Informally, in the lounge at night over a cup of tea, I'm sure they do share. But that can also be a problem because they've got so much of their own baggage that to have a woman off-load onto them can be too much. Really that's what we're here for, they should be off-loading to us. We're trained and we're objective.'

There but for the grace of God go I

We asked how the project worker copes with a job that she admits can be emotionally and even physically draining. 'Like any work where you're helping people, you tend to think you're really lucky. There but for the grace of God go I. I think that every day, and the other workers do too. A woman comes in with two children and she's had these awful experiences over ten years and I think, "I could have chosen the wrong partner and that could have happened to me." You tend to become quite cynical and hard and I think that's really a coping mechanism. But every day things touch you and it's just being there for the person when they need you. I feel good on the advice line just being there for the hour to give a woman what she hasn't had and listen to her and say, "We're here for you." And sometimes a woman will come late on a Friday and you want to go home but she's arrived and you realize what a relief it is for her to be in a safe place and you feel, I'm glad I gave up my Friday night, getting home and going out to the pub, so that this woman can have the weekend away from her situation.'

Our second meeting with OWA staff, on 28 September 1999, took place at one of the safe houses, which was a great privilege as their whereabouts are kept strictly confidential. Another project worker had some interesting points to add to what the first had told us.

Special difficulties of women on their own

She is in charge of a house with seven bedrooms, three with single beds. 'We're fortunate that, unlike some refuges, we can take women on their own as well as families. The housing situation here in Oxford is very hard for single people, so when the women leave here they have to go into shared housing. They're in quite a vulnerable position, so to go and share a house with strangers is very difficult for them. I deal a lot, day to day, helping the women to sort out benefits, housing benefits, and housing accommodation is a huge issue, particularly for single women. When a family arrives here, fleeing from domestic violence, because they've got children the council will see them as a priority need. If they've been receiving housing benefit, while they're here they can apply for double housing benefit to cover the house they have had to leave and the cost of their accommodation here (which is priced on the basis of average Oxford prices). When they are ready to move on, they present themselves to the council as homeless. They're considered, and when they're accepted, the council will provide them with temporary accommodation, and then, if it's appropriate, with permanent accommodation. Single women can't take that route. Some councils will accept them as a priority, for having fled domestic violence; some won't. It's quite a grey area, and very stressful for the women.'

Leaving can be a hard decision

We heard that some women who come in never want to see the abusive partner again, but some can't decide whether it's right for them to come completely away. 'It's very hard for the women with children, because a lot of them feel guilty that they're taking their children out from the school, their friends, possibly family, and their fathers. So as much as the women can't stand the abuse that's going on, some of them feel it's better to have a father figure there. It might be that the father, or the stepfather, is very good with the children, but he's not with her. That is a huge emotional tie – they want to do the best for their children. A lot of women will wait and wait and wait and then when the children become involved in the abuse, they'll say "That's it. I can take it if it's me, but I can't take it if it's my children. I've had enough now." Then they come away. Maybe they'll come here for a few weeks, or a few days, and then they'll decide "No, I'm going to make another go of it." And they go back. Maybe they'll do that a few times before they realize that they need a clean break. We would totally respect their need to do that.'

'You're just a punchbag'

The second project worker vividly confirmed the first's description of the large element of control and power-seeking in the men's relationship with the women. 'We have women who come who maybe have got eating disorders or cleaning disorders. "Disorders" seems like a large word for an issue like cleaning, but sometimes they can't stop when they come into the refuge – everything's been bleached and cleaned, because they were told it wasn't good enough, by their partner, over and over, "You're not good enough, you ****." There's one woman recently who said that her husband used to say, "You're just a punchbag, you're just something to hit, that's all you're good for." Those repeated comments make them very low in their self-esteem. They start to actually lose sight of who they are, it all gets taken on board and that's what they believe.'

All kinds of women can be victims

Both project workers assured us that domestic violence affects middle-class women too, although they are more likely to be able to afford to find alternative accommodation or have friends with room to put them up. 'The whole stigma of coming to a refuge is huge, but women come here and they remain, because it's different from what they thought. They're nicely surprised, which is lovely. But women come here from a total range of backgrounds. We've had daughters here who have been attacked or abused by their fathers. We've had women who've been in lesbian relationships where they have suffered domestic violence from a female partner. It knows no bounds, it goes through each and every culture. I've talked to people outside of work, and the different reactions you get . . . some people obviously feel you're talking about something dirty, and others don't care and don't want to know, so it's just something that's brushed under the carpet, it happens behind closed doors, that's the frightening thing, how much goes on without people knowing, how much is covered up. Yes, it needs to be tackled in a big way.'

We wanted to hear more about the work OWA does with the children while they are in the refuge so we spoke to the children's officer. She told us that the school-age children all attend local schools during their stay and while they are out she has individual sessions with the mothers when they can bring up any worries about the children. Sometimes children are taking out on Mum their anger at being snatched from their familiar surroundings or they're inconsolable at leaving their pets behind.

'The hamster becomes the little thing that you can tell all your worries to and the thought that the hamster's safety might be jeopardized by leaving it at home is a big thing for children. Perhaps the child isn't talking at all, they've been deeply shocked by what they've witnessed and they could be internalizing their feelings.'

Twice a week there is a crèche for the pre-school children which gives the women time out. 'It gives them a chance to talk to their project worker and it ensures that the little ones are furthering their development in what could be a very long stay.'

Sessions with the children

After school the children can have individual sessions which help the children's officer assess how they are reacting to their situation. She described some of the frequent effects of domestic violence on children. 'Many children become very clinging and won't let Mum go anywhere without them. Others seek attention by disruptive and aggressive behaviour. Others grab a store of books and toys and scuttle off into a corner and hoard them – that is actually quite indicative of a child who's been really neglected or perhaps mistreated. There are a lot of things that we have to pick up on. It's very important for me to make my assessment really quite quickly and to get to grips with what I feel the real issues are.'

It was interesting to hear how much can be learnt from the health visitor's notes. If children are very behind on their immunizations, for instance, it may be because of reluctance to roll up sleeves and show bruises. The initial information-gathering, we heard, 'is about developing a way forward in this absolutely chaotic situation. The children can have an individual session each day if they wish. Some do, some don't want to come within a hundred miles of you. It's about trust and confidence and many have had their trust and confidence abused so much that they don't want to go anywhere near you. Some are very overfriendly and again that's worrying, it's a sign that their needs aren't being met at home. The child that comes running in and jumps on your knee and they've never met you and they're telling you that they love you and kissing and hugging you – that's very worrying. So we weigh all of these things up.'

Helping children to help themselves

Every Tuesday there is a children's meeting, bringing together the children from all three houses. 'I think that there is a strength from a shared experience that benefits the children enormously. They come in huffing and puffing, "I don't want to be here" and then never miss another one! First we have circle time, when we sit round and have juice and biscuits and just talk about how we're feeling. Many children just want to talk about how they're feeling here and now and they completely blank the past. Others only want to talk about the past and deeply resent the here and now. So you have a very strange, but important, set of dynamics! What is nice is I often find the older children become very protective of the younger ones. So a younger one might say, "I don't know what to say at school when they ask where I live, because Mummy said we can't say where we are." And I'm just about to answer when an older child says, "Don't worry, you can say you've just moved, and you're waiting for a new house and you're staying with some friends." What's so nice is that actually the children are helping themselves and I really try to say as little as possible in the meetings.'

A little toolkit

The rest of the session is devoted to therapeutic play and activities and then free play. The children's officer finds the Anti-Colouring Book very helpful – Draw your worst nightmare. Draw what you're worrying about. Draw your happiest moment. With the younger children she also uses a special puppet to help them talk about their experiences. 'What I feel very strongly is that in a way we're giving the children a little toolkit to leave with. I want them to take something away with them to make this experience a positive, meaningful one, but also to equip them with things that they can draw upon should they be in a vulnerable position again. Really the most useful thing we can do is to rekindle a sense of safety between the mother and her children. Becoming the support for these children is all well and good, but we must never replace the mother. It's about realizing the importance of keeping this family together, the importance of them being able to comfort themselves, and so empowering the women and children to be able to handle this difficult situation themselves.

Coping with a demanding job

'I think being realistic about what you can do is at the heart of coping with this job – understanding that there are limitations to what we can do to "make it all better" for people. Sharing difficulties with the team is very important and so is managing one's time so that one doesn't get worn out. But just being part of these people's lives at such a difficult time is a privilege and if at the end of a Friday afternoon you think, "What have I achieved this week?" you can nearly always leave with a sense that you have eased their pain a little bit. It's about being able to give when you feel it's needed. It's tremendously rewarding. Some days I go home and I think, "Gosh, I could never have a job where I don't have this chance to work face to face with people." I think once you've done it you almost can't go back. It's really wonderful, and I'm certainly very committed to it.'

Developing new ways of working – an integrated approach

Finally, the OWA project manager put the work of refuges into the wider context of regional and national policies and programmes. She told us that most refuges now are not only providing crisis accommodation but are also working together with other agencies such as registered social landlords, the local authorities, and housing associations, to ensure that there is a supply of housing within the public sector that women can stay at. 'I think that an adequate supply of appropriate housing is an essential requirement for the refuge movement. If you are a refuge, you want to keep the needs of the women central, cementing the ways of working you have already got, but also developing ways of working in partnership and cooperation with other agencies that provide supplementary services.

'For example we have to work quite closely with the health authority and the NHS trust and the primary care groups where doctors, nurses and midwives are becoming increasingly aware of what the needs of victims of domestic violence are. We can give them advice when it comes to actually assessing whether a woman is a victim of domestic violence or not. Sometimes medical professionals are not able to pick up signs of domestic violence. A woman who goes to the doctor may feel inhibited about mentioning domestic violence. Medical professionals are being encouraged to ask the right questions directly. The Social Services departments have got child protection policies, and we work alongside them. We also work with the Court Welfare Services in all contact arrangements for fathers to see their children. All these things are being brought together, largely because of government initiatives detailed in the document *Living Without Fear*, produced by the Women's Unit of the Home Office, which is being widely distributed.

What is it you're most afraid of?

'As far as multi-agency working goes', we were told, 'an important element is the recent Crime and Disorder Act, where community safety initiatives are being discussed by all local authorities, and all local authorities have to draw up community safety strategies. They have distributed questionnaires country-wide: "What is it you're most afraid of?" People have picked out lots of issues, but in virtually every area where the questionnaires were sent women identified violence from a partner as being something that they really feared. That is why domestic violence has got quite a lot of attention.

What will really happen?

'So the local authorities have produced these three-year action plans showing exactly how they would address issues of domestic violence: in the first instance creating awareness that it's there, and second, ensuring that people get training to be able to address domestic violence, making sure there's provision for victims of domestic violence, and making sure there's protection once they're within a safe environment. And then there's prevention, the education of young people and children still at school – everything now seems to be getting an integrated approach. The government's got grand plans with its crime reduction strategy but the resources are limited. If they say you should have more policemen on the beat, or you should have a 24-hour telephone helpline – they have to put money into it. I think that's what the Women's Aid movement is quite concerned about – the big gap between what they say they are going to do, and what is actually going to happen.

'We have been involved in working on a Thames Valley Partnership project targeting perpetrators of domestic violence, which is good but our concern is that in focusing on the men the point of view of the women should never be downplayed and they should never be coerced into attempting a process of reconciliation unless they really want it. The stress on working together on projects like this is good. Things have been done in the past, but done in isolation without letting other people know what you're doing. The new approach attempts to impress on everyone the need to co-ordinate, to work together.

Working to strict guidelines

'The other thing is the new roles, the new duties that have been placed on refuges. We're very small, we've got a limited number of spaces, so all these new policies and procedures, and monitoring arrangements and new multi-agency co-operation looks like quite a burden to us. You're always conscious that you've got to be demonstrating what you're doing to everybody: the local authority that funds you, the housing association that manages you – you've got to be accountable in a lot more ways than you used to be. Twenty years ago the Women's Aid movement was not as concerned with working to very strict guidelines, every refuge did their own thing in different ways. But we now have a Women's Aid Code of Practice which sets out very clearly what we should be doing. We are now fully affiliated to the Women's Aid Federation of England which means that there are certain things that we have to do in order to be recognized, and they provide a lot of guidance for refuges, and a lot of training.

Getting domestic violence into the mainstream

'The emphasis is on mainstreaming domestic violence so that every statutory agency needs to be considering it, not lumping it in a corner and saying, "This is the work that refuges do", which is what used to be the case. So you've got the police taking it on board with very great commitment, the health authorities and the British Medical Association have got it squarely within their remit, and the Social Services are working very hard on child protection policies and procedures. The family courts are looking at things to do with contact arrangements, where the violent partner uses the contact time to be violent again and to abuse the mother. At the end of the day, we in the refuges have to be guided by what we do best, and what we do best is providing the accommodation and the right kind of support and information for women at a time of dire need. That's why people's skills need to be constantly enhanced so that they can deliver expert help. When some kind of expert help is needed that we can't deliver, then we have to refer to other agencies.'

We felt that this increased co-operation between the statutory agencies, with domestic violence now firmly on their agenda, is a sign of hope for the future. Likewise, the sad stories of the physical and emotional abuse suffered by women and children are balanced by the hope offered by the dedicated workers at OWA: listening, caring, rebuilding the women's sense of worth, 'easing their pain a little'.

~ 6 ~

New Opportunities

FULFILLING POTENTIAL – OXFORD WOMEN'S TRAINING
SCHEME (OWTS)

We heard about the OWTS from the Revd James Ramsay,
Anglican minister at the ecumenical Holy Family Church in
Blackbird Leys, a huge estate on the edge of Oxford. They kindly
invited us to go and visit and after we had been welcomed by the
scheme's manager, Jane Butcher, we were shown around some of
the classes.

Computers and carpentry

We were first taken into a computer class and explained what we
were interested in. Marigold nervously said, 'You don't have to say
anything if you'd rather not,' but when Pamela exclaimed, 'Oh,
everybody wants to say something!' everyone laughed and told us
briefly why they were there.

All the women hoped to get a good job, but were also enjoying
achieving something for themselves and becoming more helpful to
their children. Bev left school at 14 ('I could kick my own behind
for doing that'), but now aims eventually to do a four-year account-
ancy course. Barbara enjoys the companionship and the way 'you
actually feel like an individual person again.' Bagvindha feels it is
good for her children to see her doing something: 'My daughter,
she'll see me studying so then it gives her a boost.'

We then briefly dropped in on a carpentry class. The women
there stressed that you can't really live on benefits nor on the kind
of money you can earn flipping hamburgers. 'The only way you
can get a decent job is to further educate yourself.' They spoke of
the self-confidence the OWTS gives them and of how much they
appreciate the easy availability of support and advice from tutors

on any problems they may have. 'There are teachers here on the
end of a telephone if you panic.'

Later on we had the chance to talk at greater length with Kathy,
a single parent doing a computer course, and Clare, a retired
health visitor doing Manual Trades.

Kathy's story

Kathy, who left school at 16, had started by doing the Foundation
Course, which as well as introducing her to computers gave her
basic English and Maths. She then did three months on a
Women's Studies course before starting her current course toward
a BTech in computing which specializes in the technical side of
computers.

We asked Kathy what had led her to come to OWTS. 'Well, I
have two children. I'm a single parent, trapped in the benefit system. I do want to work but if I go out to work all my benefits are
reduced greatly so I'd have to be earning a lot of money to cover
that. I've been out of work a long time, bringing up my children.
I've been doing menial jobs like cleaning, but now I've got to a
stage in my life when my son is 12 and my daughter is 14 so I
thought, It's time to move on. And to get back into any office work
or anything I thought I need really to do computers, to understand
how they work and to try and improve myself. Also to meet
people. Here in college when I came to the Open Day I really liked
it. It was really relaxed and the tutors were very helpful. I did do a
course at the College of Further Education, but I didn't like it
there at all. It was completely different – mainly teenagers. Here
the people are more my age and they're in the same circumstances
as myself, so I can relate to them and I don't feel intimidated.
There are women here who can understand problems that maybe
you've got at home, so you've got somebody to talk to about it. The
tutors are very good as well.'

Kathy had felt the same sense of isolation and loneliness that we
had heard of from other single parents. 'People have said to me,
when there are times I've been lonely, "How can you be lonely?
You've got two kids." But you are. It's a completely different company than what you would get from a partner. It is very difficult

bringing up children on your own. Here you're getting a lot of support, not only for things you're studying, but also for any problems at home. It's very good.'

Like so many OWTS students, Kathy is hoping to go on to further studies. 'I've been thinking that maybe I wouldn't mind going to Ruskin College because they've got a Women's Studies course. Coming here has made me feel there are things I *can* do.' Her self-confidence has also spread into other areas of her life. 'I was decorating my living-room, and a friend of mine, a man, said, "Who moved all the furniture, and who did this, and who did that?" and I said, "Well, I did it!" I've lived on my own for seven years so there's lots of things that you have to be able to do yourself. You can't rely on somebody else to do it for you. You find that you have to cope and it's made me a lot stronger. Coming here has given me more confidence – I just wish I'd come years earlier. I shall be sorry to leave actually. I keep thinking, "Can't I do a further course here?' I'm always promoting it when I go out and see people."

Clare's story

Clare is another enthusiast for OWTS courses. She is a retired health visitor and is now in her third term of Manual Trades. She started with the general Multiskills course and went on to introductory woodwork. 'You have to do several projects: first you have to make a little bench-hook so you can do your sawing straight. Then we did an architrave of a door, and then we did a little bookcase. I did one that you could put three rows of cassettes on and I'm so proud of it.' Clare hopes, in September, to start a year's course in painting and decorating with a view to helping people who need decorating done but can't do it themselves. 'I haven't got the initiative or the drive now to want to do that sort of thing as a business,' she told us. But it was evident that she is in fact full of initiative and a desire to be of service in her retirement. It emerged that she had heard about OWTS because she already knew one of the tutors– the two of them had been mentors for lone parents, helping them to get back to work. And last summer holidays she had spent a month in Belize helping to build a Health Centre. 'I did mostly sweeping up because it was very physical, very, very hot (over 101°F) and also very humid when the hurricanes began. But it gave me a very good start for here!'

A tutor's eye view

Liz Sheeron, one of the computer tutors and a member of the OWTS management team, kindly took time out of her lunch break to talk with us about the courses and the participants. She told us about the kind of circumstances which lead women to come to the OWTS. 'I think that quite a lot of women come here because there's a change in their life. They may split up from their partner, or their children have got to an age that they're going to school and because of that they make a decision to do something. Women who split from a partner need to do two things: they need to generate their own income, if they haven't been doing that already, and they've also got something to prove. Usually they want to *show* their partner. They think, "I'll show him I can do this", and then it starts being, "Well, I'm going to do this for me." And that is life-changing. Whether it's in computers or in manual trades, these women are proving that they can get a job and that they are worth something. You see some women coming in here who don't have any self-worth and that's dreadful. And they do very good things here. It takes a while for them to realize that, and that they do have something to offer, because they're used to being told at home that they're no good.'

A success story

Liz told us about one student who had had very little work experience and had a very limited expectation of what she was going to achieve. 'Academically she wasn't great, but she was very good practically. She did a work placement which didn't work out – they didn't really get on with her and she didn't get on with them and it was all not very good. Then she did another work placement and she just took to it like a duck to water. It was very practical – she was taking computers apart and mending them, she was installing software, she was installing hardware. And now she's employed permanently as a junior systems engineer and she's doing great. From coming in expecting very little, not knowing what she wanted to do, she found something she was good at and she knew she was good at it. Those kind of things are wonderful. That's a success story.'

At the time of our visit there were two foundation courses running, with about nine students in each; three vocational courses with between six and nine in each and a technical course with four students. We heard that one of the most popular courses is Computing with Language Support which is for students who need support with English. 'The women who come may have recently arrived in the country so they learn computing skills and they get support with their English. It's difficult to do a computing course without a certain amount of English because of the jargon and following instructions.' Other women may have been in England for many years but have not developed English language skills because of isolation in the home and family setting.

We learnt that the funding for OWTS comes mainly from Oxford City Council and the European Social Fund plus a contribution from the government's Single Regeneration Fund which covers the outreach work. OWTS belongs to the national Women's Training Network. The courses are free to women who meet the criteria and contributions are made towards travel and childcare. 'Some people have to travel by train to get here. And we've got one student, she's only young and she's got five kids and if she had to pay for childcare it would just rule it out. Once the children are in school it's a bit more sensible for her to look for employment, so she's preparing for that moment. The cost of childcare is tremendous and that's one of the things that women who leave here have to consider, because the cost of a childminder can be more than what they're earning, so that can affect when they feel able to take a job.'

The support given by the tutors impressed us greatly and is obviously a very important element in the success stories we heard about. 'Each student is assigned a certain amount of tutorial support during their course, so that they can talk about their work and their progress and any problems they may have that might affect their work. If they wanted to talk about something that needed expertise, we'd direct them to doctors or to counsellors or various organizations. Through the tutorial support, they can bring things to our attention that they might not feel able to bring up in class. They might want to make a criticism or they might just want to go over something.'

Passing on skills and encouragement to others

We were very keen to hear the stories of two staff members who started their careers by doing courses at OWTS and are now passing on to other women the skills and the self-confidence which they learnt there. One cannot imagine better role models than these two dynamic women.

First story

'I'm a black woman who returned to education about five or six years ago, because I just needed a change really. As a lone parent I felt I needed to break the cycle of being on income support and be able to support myself, so I started a computer course at the OWTS. I did the Foundation Course and then the BTech and soon after that the job of Education Development Worker came up and the tutors encouraged me to go for it. I had really wanted something computer-based but this job seemed quite exciting because it was work with people, getting people in the same situation I'd been in to come back into education. That for me was a challenge. I thought it was going to be easy, but it's not always that easy because people are at different stages in their lives. It might take them a year or two years to come back after talking to me. They don't all say, "Oh yes, that sounds fantastic! I'm going to do that", which I thought they would – a bit naïve really!

'My job is to go round trying to get people interested, finding out what women want to do and seeing if the OWTS can develop courses to suit them. Many women's initial reaction to working a computer is "I can't do that!" But they want to be able to help their children, or else they think that if they can use a word-processor they can get an office job. But once they get here, they seem to start aiming higher, because it empowers them to do something they never thought they would be able to achieve. And it's fantastic when you see that. It was fantastic for me meeting all these different women who'd been at home like me thinking, "What can I do? I can't really do much." Here they start by going through all the things you *can* do: if you're a mum at home you have to work out how much money you're going to spend on food, so that's working out how to use money. You've actually got a lot of transferable skills you can use. We work on those and people start feeling better about themselves, gaining confidence, and that's what it's about really.

'That's what helped me. While I was here doing my studying, a tutor said to me, "You'll be good at teaching", because if I finished my work I would go and help other people without being prompted. I'm now doing a City and Guilds course in teaching adults. I've completed Stage 1, I'm currently on Stage 2 and then I'm aiming for a Certificate of Education at Oxford Brookes University. I like the job I'm doing now, getting people back into education, but I also like teaching and seeing people progress and giving them power to do things. I definitely think I'm a people person – you can stick me in a room with all ages and in five minutes I'll be chatting away. So I'm not afraid of those situations. Paperwork's my downfall! I'll have to get a secretary!'

Life in Blackbird Leys

Although there are quite a lot of black families in Blackbird Leys, we were told that there is no such thing as a separate black community and people mix quite happily. She contrasts this with the situation of her cousins in London. 'It happens in a lot of communities, you don't mix with white people unless you're working with them, whereas I socialize with anyone really. I've got friends of all different nationalities, so I've got different ideas, I've been to different places, but they're in a black community. They might as well be in Jamaica. My cousins came down from London to my son's christening and they were shocked that there were so many blacks and whites mixed in the room, because in London if you went to a christening it would be nearly all black people, totally different.

'I help to run an African Caribbean Women's Group where

black women come to talk about their concerns and in the recent annual Oxford International Women's Festival (during which the OWTS held an Open Day) the Group sponsored a play called *Sea Change – Three Generations of Black Women in Oxford*, followed by discussion. During the 1999 festival the Group held a discussion group for black women. We talked about books and poetry and about cooking. People were saying what was their favourite poem and reading it. We discussed what books were good to read and that sort of thing, so it was just a normal women's group. We don't necessarily talk about "black issues" like, for instance, a white couple adopting a black child. People have been saying that's not right, but a white couple may be more in tune with black issues than a black couple. That's my opinion, maybe because I'm not really up on black issues – maybe I should be.'

Marigold said she couldn't see any reason for just concentrating on black issues. 'I know,' was the response, 'but people assume that you know about this and that because you're black, and I'm afraid I don't. I think I'm a lot more English than I thought! I'm very westernized because I've been brought up in a totally western society, so I don't know anything else.'

She came to Britain when she was seven. Her parents had left her with her grandparents when they came here to work and when she arrived she found she had three brothers (only one of whom she already knew) and another on the way. 'I was the eldest so all the responsibility was on my shoulders. England was strange, everything was massive, all these old buildings – and the cold! It was a bit of a culture shock. I went to school and didn't really get on that brilliantly. I was a bit of a clown because I didn't want people to see how I was feeling. You have to pretend everything's happy when it's not.' She found it hard often being the only black girl in her class. 'When I got to secondary school there was one other black girl in my class and when they talked about certain subjects, slavery for instance, it felt uncomfortable. I think I would have preferred to go to a school where there was a mixture. I always stood out. It was good and bad. I think it's helped me in a way because I'm not just in a black mindset. I'm open to all kinds of things, whereas had I gone to a mostly black school I might not have got those opportunities. That's the other side of the coin.'

Nowadays she is a governor at her son's school, having previously been a governor at her daughter's. 'I like to keep in touch with the school and how education is going, so that my son gets a good start. I definitely think if you're involved with the school, you do get a better deal. I know that it shouldn't work like that, but if you get to know the teachers and headmistress they can see you're interested, so they'll take an interest in your child, and you'll know every time your child does something, which can be annoying sometimes! I just want to make sure that he gets what I didn't, because I know it's difficult. It's worse if you've got boys, because I think boys tend to be stereotyped easier than girls. I think black boys are more likely to hang round in groups with other black boys and that can look like a problem even if it isn't really. I remember at school if there were four black people together it was seen as ganging. If you saw four white children together you wouldn't think they were forming a gang, would you? I'm always trying to break the stereotype.'

A friend runs a homework club for underachieving black or mixed race boys. 'There's also a Saturday school which I think is open to anyone now, but it started for black and mixed race children. Sometimes I think there's a danger in doing that because you're excluding people. *We* talk about being excluded, *we're* being excluded, and then we're doing the same thing! I just think things should be mixed.'

Second story

Our second storyteller was born in England and grew up in Blackbird Leys. She was happy at school and was not conscious of any colour barrier between herself and her classmates. But looking back on her schooldays she has realized that she was in fact treated differently by the teachers. 'I think if your parents aren't from England and don't know the system you just go along with the flow and get stuck in a box because you don't realize that if you do that little bit more you can do different things. Maybe the school didn't think that your parents were interested so you were left to your own devices and at the end you realize, "Well, if I'd known, I'd have done that." When it came to choosing options for jobs, I chose things that I thought were fun. I wasn't encouraged to choose things I was getting really good grades in like physics and chemistry. I had no career guidance whatsoever. Nobody took the time to know me as an individual or to know one black child from another. I had a friend who I used to go around with, and they'd constantly get us muddled up. I knew we weren't allowed out of school at lunch-time, but she'd go off to the chippy, and it was always me that was pulled into the office. They couldn't tell us apart, and we look nothing alike! In the end I asked to be moved out of her class but I still got blamed for things she was doing.'

She went to a College of Further Education and did a certificate in residential and social care. The student teaching element of that made her wish she could go into teaching but she needed to start earning so at the age of 18 she went to work in an old people's home. She spent the first two weeks crying and vowing she would *never* get old, but soon came to love the work. At 21 she had her first child and stopped work for a while before ending up at OWTS doing a BTech in computing. 'I remember after having my daughter I couldn't hold an adult conversation with anybody, it was just child, child, child! I could feel myself wanting to kick myself – Will you stop talking about that child for one minute! And it wasn't that I wanted to keep speaking about her, it was that I had nothing else to say. The course was fantastic, the relationships and friends that you met, and the things that you started to do. I was offered a job at my work placement and that was a nice way to get back into working. But I did lots of other jobs, I was always doing two jobs at a time, one was never enough money for what I needed to survive. So the OWTS was my step to where I was going. I was never going to look back.'

After a number of other jobs, two more children and various courses and part-time jobs at the OWTS ('They can't get rid of me!'), she was staggered and thrilled to be offered a teaching job at an Adult Education Centre. 'It was a real shock because although I was used to helping people my own age when we were doing the same course, I never thought I could actually go out and earn money doing it somewhere else. But I always did want to teach, and I knew there was something I could actually pass on to somebody else.' She is now in her second year of teacher-training and still teaching part-time. 'I've got a lot from all my training and now I feel I'm giving something back. It's a really good feeling to have 100% of your students pass in two courses. When they arrive they're so nervous, and by the time they've finished they're saying, "I'm going to go off and do this, or I'm looking for another course and I'm coming back to you next time."

'I had one lot who actually refused to start a course on its next due day because they wanted to wait until I was doing it. I said, "No, my friend's doing it, she's really good", but they wouldn't go. They said, "No, we'll wait until you're doing it and we'll come back because we know you now, and we know how you work." That was such a nice compliment for me. I know that I can do whatever I put my mind to, but sometimes I don't actually believe it. "Oh gosh! Did I really do that? Did I really just get 23 people through the exam? What would my teachers think now?"

FROM STEELWORKER'S DAUGHTER TO ADULT EDUCATION PROMOTER

Jo Forster not only arranged meetings for us in the North-East but put us up for three nights in her home in Whitley Bay. One evening she told us her own story, which started in a two-up, two-down in Consett, then dominated by the steelworks where her father worked all his life. 'We had a coal-house and a toilet in the backyard and an air-raid shelter left over from the war. My aunts and uncles all lived in the same street and we helped each other out if we ran out of sugar or something before payday. My mother, a lay Franciscan, spent a lot of time working in the community, caring for the sick. If someone died she'd be called upon to dress the body.'

Consett in the old days

Jo's mother spent the last ten years of her life at the Rosemount Nursing Home and one afternoon we went to Consett to talk with some of the residents about their memories and the changes brought about by the closure of the steelworks in 1980. Like Jo, they remembered waking to the sound of steelworkers' boots clumping past, but one lady remembered her house being bolted and barred when they came past after going to the pub on a Saturday night. 'If our mother and father went out we had a poker and a wire hairbrush behind the front door!' Some went back to very early days with talk of diphtheria and scarlet fever epidemics, horse-drawn ambulances and hospitals putting three children in two beds. The community spirit was strong, centred largely on the worship and social gatherings of the churches.

Everything depended on the steelworks and its demise was a great blow, though no one misses the pervasive red dust it generated. Jobs in the new small industries are mainly for women and young people have to move away to find work. The loss of the popular Saturday market was much regretted and the ladies were loud in their condemnation of the effect on the town of 'planning', which had lost them some of its best roads and parks, and destroyed any character the town had.

Jo's journey

At age 11, Jo went to the convent school but left at 16 when her father retired and there was no money for her to continue her education. She went to work at the Labour Exchange and in 1972 married John. 'I never expected to marry an Oxford graduate, or have a public school life in Tynemouth [John is Head of Sixth Form Studies at Kings School, Tynemouth], or any of those kind of aspirations. I had been brought up to have a large family and live a basic life with a steelworker. At times I think I'm out of my depth, the things that have happened to me. I didn't ever expect to have what I've got or how I live, or my education, or anything.' Jo continued working until the birth of her first child when she heard about a New Opportunities for Women course run by Newcastle University and was accepted for a course on English and Politics which earned her a credit towards going to university. When her second daughter started school she acquired another credit in English and Philosophy and an A-level in Religious Studies, going on to obtain a degree in Theology at Newcastle University.

Back to square one

With no better job appearing, Jo went back to the Labour Exchange, where her new boss put her back on the bottom rung. After six months pinning cards on boards Jo appealed, got her executive status back and became a Staff Development Officer training the counsellors who work in the inner city offices. She also helped them to develop diagnostic skills in order to identify applicants' problems and direct them towards appropriate adult education. 'It hadn't happened before because the employment service was a very narrow organization. It thought there was just one way, and that was not training, not education, but just telling people about jobs, and if they didn't get them, well they weren't any good. The courses I designed became national courses for the employment service.' Jo went on to research and design the first Open Learning Centre for the Department of Employment, for which she won an award. She also found time to produce a Masters thesis, 'Good News for the Poor', on how the methodology of liberation theology could be used with people in this country who have literacy problems.

The world of work

'I've encountered all kinds of problems and hassles and conflicts that I don't find easy to handle in the world of work. It's a very complex place, full of power struggles and fighting and conflicts and aspirations. And the community gets lost in it. I feel I'm very much there to focus back on the community. But if you open your mouth you won't get promotion, you'll get hassle or you'll be pulled in and told to keep quiet. And I can't do that because I feel that my purpose is to awaken awareness on the issues of the poor and the community, and the needs of the community. We live in a democracy, so people have to have a choice in what happens to them, and very often that choice is taken away by councillors who are supposed to be working for the people. I don't aim to make myself popular, a lot of people can't stand me because I tell the truth, and they don't like it.'

God's plan

Looking back over the unexpected directions her life had taken, Jo commented, 'I suppose God has a plan for you, but you've got to respond and take what you're called to do, haven't you? Try to make the right decisions. I've made a lot of mistakes, I've got plenty of bruises. But I have a very centred prayer life and eucharistic life, and a rosary life. It's very traditional I know, but it's very essential and integral to my survival.'

(Jo tells us she has now retired and is doing voluntary work for seven different organizations!)

EMPOWERING THROUGH MICRO-CREDIT

Jennifer Kavanagh welcomed us in her Tower Hamlets office next to the handsome church which the Unitarians had offered to Quaker Social Action to turn into a Community Centre. Jennifer, having sold her literary agency, first took on the job as a volunteer.

A great culture shock

'I knew nothing about the voluntary sector, I knew nothing about the area, I felt green beyond belief. To begin with I was terrified of walking through the estate in the dark, and now I never think about it. I cycled round the area for three weeks, trying to get to know what was going on, where the gaps were, what we ought to do, what people wanted us to do. This is the fifth most deprived ward in the country – bits of Bethnal Green are coming up in the world, but this particular bit is very deprived. It has a very large Bangladeshi community, many of whom don't speak English; there are a lot of very isolated women at home; a lot of over-crowding; there's a higher incidence of disability in Tower Hamlets than practically anywhere else in the country, and a very high rate of unemployment. You name it, on all the indices it scores very highly.'

A thriving Centre develops

After a slow start and with few financial resources, things began to happen, and the Centre soon became a hive of activity. 'We started a parents and toddlers group. We have a wonderful women's group which runs itself: they have keep fit classes, reflexology, and we've now got a girls' keep fit class going, because there are a lot of Bangladeshi girls here who are not allowed to go anywhere unless it's thoroughly vetted. We've started community meals for isolated people. This has meant an amazing growth in confidence for our two cooks, one Bangladeshi, the other North African, and it has taught the community the pleasures of eating together. There's a pensioners' bowls team. We've now got £20,000 European money to spend on updating the building, and we're applying for more for disabled access.'

Micro-credit for women, run by women

About a year ago it had become apparent that some sort of financial intervention was necessary to give local people a 'kick-start', so Quaker Social Action embarked on a micro-credit scheme, which Jennifer could run in the three days a week she works for QSA. She gave up running the Centre and now concentrates on the micro-credit project 'Street Cred'. 'The way we're doing it is for women only, for women who are unemployed on very low income, who cannot access funds from anywhere else, who have an idea about self-employment, and who are prepared to form groups to support each other. They must guarantee each other's loan, and take responsibility for each loan. So you are dealing with people who are on benefit, moving from receiving money to receiving a loan which they have to pay back – and this is quite a different mindset. We lend a maximum of £500 for a sewing machine, or enough food to get a cooking scheme off the ground, or enough material to get dressmaking started, or a computer, or a camera, or whatever it is, but it's for a specific capital item. The idea is that they start something very small from home, which for a lot of women is the only possibility, because their husbands wouldn't approve of them working anywhere else. Then they might be able to sell through a stall, or a shop. Some enterprises will always be tiny, others will blossom.'

Jennifer was clearly very much at home in the East End. 'It's exciting, it's challenging! I really enjoy it, the variety, the friendliness, the down-to-earthness. It's good.'

The homeless have minds as well

With her other hat on, as clerk of Quaker Homeless Action (a different charity that acts nationally, but mostly in central London), Jennifer and the QHA team had just set up a mobile library for homeless people. 'I put a letter in *The Bookseller* asking for books and we got about 2,500. We've got 20 volunteers and a van, two of us go out every Saturday morning to prearranged stops (near hostels and Day Centres in the Victoria area and the back of St Martin in the Fields one week, Waterloo and Parker Street off Kingsway the next). We launched it at our Christmas shelter, and we started out on the road in January. We're lending about 30 books a week, and it's gradually growing. I went out on Saturday and we had three absolute regulars, who started at Christmas and have come every fortnight since, because we do it in two different places, alternate weeks. I had a great chat with them – it's lovely, because it's them saying to the world, "We are your intellectual equals – we have minds as well as needing shelter." When we go out on the food runs we don't have as much time, there are more people. I've had real in-depth discussions through the library. We're also trying to find a programme for two illiterate people and we expect to be dealing with other problems too.'

SOMETHING CREATIVE FOR MUMS

Sculptor Olympia Sutherland is resident artist in charge of The Ark–T Tuesday Art Group at the John Bunyan Baptist Church in Cowley, Oxford. A Peruvian painter, Ernesto Uzuriaga, is resident artist and curator of the gallery. The minister, James Grote, had wanted to bring in the local community, so he opened up a part of the church complex which had been under-used and made it into a Centre for all sorts of activities.

We met Olympia in the large hall where the group were busily painting, and she told us how she had got involved with the project. 'I got involved with this project for purely selfish reasons – I was looking for studio space for my own work! James and Ernesto were talking about how important it would be to bring people into the Centre through the arts, an outreach to the community, and I found this very exciting. There was a toddler group here which met twice a week, and we thought that the mums might be interested in doing something creative.

'It's an open art group, you come along when you can, the children can play and the mums have a chance for an hour or so to do something for themselves, which can be quite therapeutic. The art can be confidence boosting as well; the role of mother is an incredibly important one, but I think in motherhood sometimes one's confidence in one's own self-worth can suffer maybe, because you're giving all the time.'

The women coming to the art group are from a variety of backgrounds and experiences, and are united in their enthusiasm for their painting and their appreciation of Olympia's respectful, non-judgemental attitude to their work.

Lesley has two children, and was finishing a PhD in engineering. 'I first came to the group two weeks ago, and I was so excited I worked at full-rate the whole time, and I couldn't calm down when I got home. It's not often I do something for myself, it's always the children. It's nice to feel a bit more of a whole person rather than just a mum.'

Jane was ordained five years ago as an Anglican priest. Her husband is also a priest; they both work part-time and share the childcare. Jane does a lot of counselling and she commented, 'One of the lovely things about being here is that it's a chance for me to express *my* emotions. When you're dealing with a lot of people who have very acute emotions, you're there for them – and this is a place that's here for me and my emotions and where I'm at as a person.'

Lynn studied physics at university and felt that her creative side was undeveloped until, after her children were born, she started to paint. 'I found it both deeply frustrating and deeply releasing, partly because I could never create something that both looked nice *and* expressed what I wanted to say! Coming to the art group the two things started to come together. One of the things I find

really exciting is looking at the link between creativity and prayer
– how strong that is, and how very often it is in allowing yourself
to have freedom just to create for the sake of it, that you can
release the greatest creativity. And the kids have just loved it. I'm
giving them space to do that within themselves, and they will very
often paint to express what they want to say, either to God, or
occasionally in a prophetic sense. It seems to flow very naturally
between their own self-understanding and their sensitivity of
spirit. There doesn't seem to be that dividing line between the
two.'

Rosaleen works part-time as a research fellow in a psychology
department, her field being discourse analysis in social psychology.
'I'm finding it quite difficult to reconcile myself to how cold-
hearted it can seem at times, because it's an academic discipline.
But lately I've started painting at home. It's increasingly important
to me, it's something that I've put on the back burner most of my
life. I've done what I should do, or what I felt I should do, but it
hasn't been in tune with what I feel I need. I've had a bereavement
recently, somebody who was slightly younger than me. And I
thought, "Well, get on with it! Just get on with it and do it while
there's time." And here I am.'

Sonja saw the art group advertised and thought it was something she could do for herself. 'I never did anything with glass
painting, and I felt quite interested to see how I would do it. It is
slippery, and I thought, "How would you paint on glass? How
would it look?"' Sonja felt strongly that they were trying to dis-
credit art in schools. 'My daughter's doing GCSE and the teacher
asked, "Why do you want to take A Level art?" I think it's all wrong,
because art is something in you, it's your soul. You wouldn't criticize people for writing a book, so why do you criticize people for
doing art?'

Sculpting hope and optimism

Olympia showed us some of her sculptures and said Hope had
been the theme. 'It's been about rebirth and new life and hope and
forward motion. About a year ago I was making the pod form,
seed form, with little growing shoots. It was a symbol of my new

life as a Christian, having come back to faith. Now I'm using the female form as a symbol for potential growth or creativity or new life and nurture.'

Olympia later held an exhibition of her work in the small Ark–T gallery attached to the church. It had developed from stone carving into fabric and plaster modelling, still expressing the concept of hope. 'It is this state of hope I wish to continue exploring through as many materials as possible, with reference to symbols, objects and the human figure. My aim is to produce work with a conscience, work with social responsibility, work that seeks to nurture a positive transaction with the viewer.'

～ 7 ～

Ministers' Wives and Women Ministers

The days when it could be said that doing the flowers in church and making the tea 'can safely be left to the ladies, God bless them' are over. The women in this chapter are living witnesses to that fact, and in the stories that follow we see them breaking away from the stereotypes and challenging outdated mindsets.

NEW LIFE IN A METHODIST CHURCH

We had first met Mary Jefferson in connection with our El Salvador book, which was reviewed in *Magnet*, the inspiring publication of the Methodist Women's Network, with which she is very active. She, and her husband, Derek, a retired minister, kindly hosted part of our stay in Sheffield.

When Derek and Mary decided to leave the posh suburb of Sheffield where they lived, and move into the inner city, they thought they were being rather good. 'But it wasn't like that at all. Coming here has been a whole new experience. It was just wonderful! It is still just wonderful living here and being part of this community.' To give us a taste of the community, after supper Mary took us round the corner to the weekly house group meeting in the home of her friend Vicky, where we also met two other West Indian women, Miriam and Thelma. (Forty per cent of the membership of the Victoria Church to which Mary belongs now comes from the Afro-Caribbean community.)

We didn't like the welcome

Vicky arrived in 1961, Miriam in 1959 and Thelma in 1958 and all started by working at Lodge Moor Hospital. Vicky did domestic work, which she had never done before. Her husband had no job then so her £7 weekly wage had to pay the rent, feed them and help support a child back home. Miriam was a nursing auxiliary, first at Lodge Moor, then at Nether Edge, for 25 years and really enjoyed it. 'You get to know different types of people. I get on so well with them and all my patients they miss me when I'm not there. I just do to them as I would like them to do to me if I was in their place.' Thelma started at Lodge Moor but then worked in transport for 25 years, first as a conductress, then cleaning buses, which paid better. All said it was their faith that got them through the hard times though they had not found the welcome they had hoped for in the church. 'When we used to go at first', said Vicky, 'we were glad to get in and get out, because we didn't like the welcome. I was frightened to go. Sometimes we'd sit at the back and then rush off, but it's a lot different now. Now we can have a little chat with whoever's there, we don't rush to come home.'

Miriam said there was a big change even on the streets, 'They get to know that we're only human like them, and we get to know the same – it works both ways.' She told us that in the church the big change had come with the arrival of Mark Kellett as minister. 'It's a lot better now, because you're all sisters and brothers there now. We don't have anybody saying, "Shall we go in?" You go in now, and you're all right. It's all God's doing.' Thelma agreed. 'God always provides. He doesn't put knife and fork and plate at table, but he provides.'

Mary's story

Mary had always felt that teaching was her vocation. Now retired, she had taught in schools and teacher training colleges and at retirement was an advisory inspector of schools. 'God has always been part of my awareness, but it was a very closed-in awareness. It wasn't until I left home and went to university, where I was part of an ecumenical group in the Student Christian Movement, that I began to think, and question all kinds of things about my faith.'

'I wanted to be me'

Mary's post-university plans changed when she married Derek, and adjusting to her new role was not easy. 'I had a job, and

ministers' wives didn't have jobs in those days. I realized that
people expected me to be the stereotypical minister's wife, there to
do what the minister and the local church wanted her to do. I
wanted to back Derek up, but I didn't quite fit the role. I wanted
to be me. I was sure that God wanted me to be me, and Derek
encouraged me.' Also, in those days Methodist ministers moved on
about every three years. Derek found it exciting but Mary hated
leaving her friends.

Shouting at God

'Why have we got to move?' Mary shouted at God. But having
children made a huge difference. 'It was a whole new step in knowing God and finding God at work in my body as well as in their
lives. Bringing up children is the hardest thing I've ever tried to do.
It takes all your faith. And yet somehow God is in it all the time. I
suppose the hardest time for us all was when our son was killed by
an avalanche in Peru. That was very hard to come to terms with.
I could not find God at that stage. I really yelled at God then. We
went to Peru and the people we met were amazing. People were
the way I found God then, it was other people who were God to
me.'

CHRIS KELLETT – ADJUSTING TO WIDOWHOOD

At Mary's house we met Chris, widow of the minister Mark,
praised by Miriam, who had recently died. They had always
moved around a lot, when Mark was a civil engineer and after he
became a Methodist minister. 'So when Mark died, in a way it was
another new situation such as I had been used to coping with,
except that I was not used to coping on my own. Once more I'm
having to find out what I can do in this new situation, what contribution I can make. I'm waiting for guidance to see where I go
from here.'

To Jamaica and back

Like Mary Jefferson, Chris resisted taking on the role of a stereotypical minister's wife. 'I didn't see myself opening bazaars and
running women's meetings. I saw myself as wife to my husband,

supporting him in his work, whether he was a civil engineer or a minister, and of course bringing up the children.' During their five years in Jamaica Chris practised as a doctor and was also organist and choir mistress in the church. Returning to the UK was a culture shock. 'We went up to Northumberland, having never before lived in an all-white area, or a relatively affluent area. The people were very nice but their experience of the sort of things we were talking about was very limited, as was our experience of the things that mattered to them. When I first arrived people came up, very friendly, and said things like, "Hello, do you like baking?" and I'd say, "No", and there was no more conversation! Once they were aware of problems, they were very good and very generous – they supported the church in Jamaica and the homeless venture in Newcastle – but within their own community their experience was very limited and I found that hard.'

Return to Sheffield

Mark knew he was ill before they left Northumberland and they experienced tremendous support from everyone back in Sheffield. Chris felt they had been led there. 'In my life I can look back and see God's hand. I've very rarely been conscious of him pushing me but once we'd made the decision to come I was so overwhelmingly at peace, I knew it was the right thing to do. Mark knew what was wrong with him and what the prognosis was, and being able to talk about things and be open with everybody has been wonderful. We were able to do a lot of our grieving before he died, which was very good. But also we were able to have a lot of joy and happiness, with lots of family gatherings and laughter and parties with friends.'

Church – a different language?

Chris felt that, strangely, all this had been a very positive experience in many ways. She remembered a friend who had cancer and said she was upheld on a carpet of prayer. 'I can say that is how we felt.' Chris had met people with no faith who had experienced bereavement, and wondered how they coped. 'I often think people have faith but have no language to describe their faith, because they're not church people. We tend to think if you're not a church person you have no faith, but a lot of people, when moments of crisis come, feel there is something else there. But the Church hasn't managed to help them explore this feeling. "If you're not one of us . . ."' In Jamaica, allegiance to the Church as well as to God was a normal part of life. 'But here,' Chris said, 'where church people are in such a minority, "church" is almost a dirty word in some parts of society. I feel very strongly that the Church has got totally out of touch with what people are wanting. But people out there are still looking for something, wanting something.' Chris and Mark had had tremendous support from the Macmillan team looking after Mark. 'They are trained to talk to people, but even so we had far deeper conversations with them than we did with a lot of church people who came, and I don't know that either of them went to church. Maybe in church we use a different language.'

THE CURRENT MINISTER OF VICTORIA CHURCH – ANNE GIBSON

Before becoming a minister, Anne had been a principal social worker in Liverpool. After a theology degree at Wesley House in Cambridge she went to Wesley College in Bristol where, besides teaching New Testament, she had pastoral responsibilities for students and their families.

The token woman

'That experience was both difficult and enriching. I probably learnt more there, in the classroom and in the staff room, than I did in my own training. I was the only woman on the staff – I'd gone there because they wanted a woman on the staff – so there was a bit about being the token woman, which was quite hard. For the first time, I became aware of the situation of women in the Church and more aware of feminist issues. I realized that a lot of women's experience of themselves, their lives and their bodies, is not somehow embraced into our thinking about God and the way God works in the world. The students ranged from the very evangelical, charismatic and fundamentalist, to the liberal and radical. It was a challenging time.'

Formative experience in Africa

A further mind-changing experience came when Anne had the opportunity to go on an exchange with a black male Methodist minister from a seminary in Pietermaritzburg, South Africa, and taught for a term at a largely black seminary. She saw the effects of oppression and racism, and how in large parts of the white Church, Christianity had been spiritualized 'off the face of the earth'. 'I remember going to a conference where the white ministers talked about demons, meaning evil powers, but did not look at the real evil in their society.'

They had died and risen again

Anne came back to Bristol for another two terms before going into circuit in Birmingham, where she was part of a Local Ecumenical Partnership. 'That was a very exciting place to be, where three churches, Anglican, Methodist and URC, had come together into one, been welded into one congregation. They had all died and risen again. It was an open, lively, thriving building, serving the local community. The Anglican and URC churches were sold and they all came together in the refurbished Methodist building as one worshipping community.'

God was laughing up her sleeve!

Anne is involved with several churches in Sheffield, but Victoria, a 700-seater building built at the turn of the last century is the main one. There are plans to develop the church for multi-purpose use. 'There's a vision to make the place serve the community and the neighbourhood. I spent seven years in Birmingham saying, "Thank God I arrived when this building was all sorted out", but I think God was laughing up her sleeve the whole time, because I ended up here with *this* building to tangle with!'

'Follow, follow Jesus'

Anne had a strong sense of being called to this particular place and this particular work. 'As we were singing that song at the Fun Day, "Follow, follow Jesus", I thought, "Well, yes, he's led me a long way from where I first began", and I feel enormously privileged to have had this opportunity. Although I never thought to be a minister, and although I feel that in many ways I could have continued to serve the Kingdom of God as a social worker, it just so happened that I was called to something different at that point in time.'

The creative ministry of women

Anne is a superintendent Methodist minister, one of only three in the Sheffield District of the Methodist Church, with some responsibility for the circuit. 'I think there has been a lot of progress in the Methodist Church, since women have been ordained now over 25 years, but many would argue there is still a long way to go. There are a lot more women offering for ministry now, and I do feel that women have such a creative ministry and do bring something different in all walks of life, but in this one particularly.'

ANGLICAN MINISTRY IS BRILLIANT!

Rachel Wadey was ordained a deacon in the Church of England in June 1998 and a priest in July 1999. She is now a curate in Poulton-le-Fylde, Lancashire, an area which had not encountered an ordained female before. She has kept her membership of the Society of Friends and occasionally manages to attend a midweek meeting for worship in Blackpool.

To Brazil and back

When Marigold first met Rachel she was a Quaker school-leaver about to go and work for six months with children in a *favela* in Recife, Brazil. How did she come to be an Anglican priest? 'In Recife I worked with a woman who belonged to the Church of England but who also worked closely with the Roman Catholics, and I came to admire her spirituality and to love the liturgies. It was she who first suggested that I might have a vocation for the ministry.' Back home, she explored various possible ministries, including teaching and nursing, 'But none of them had that feeling of being the right thing for me to do. So I carried on looking at ordination. I thought the university chaplain at Lancaster would say, "Don't be daft", but instead he put me in touch with the vocations staff in the diocese and it just went from there.'

Testing it out

During that time Rachel spent a year working in a parish on a council estate in Liverpool, 'I suppose', she said, 'to test out whether I enjoyed it because I thought that if you believe God wants people to have quality of life and fullness of life then it should be possible to enjoy what you do as part of your faith. I was a bit wary, I suppose, that when you're ordained you have to age to being about 45 and go into flowery print dresses and stuff like that, which isn't very me! Luckily I worked with two young curates who were very much their own people, and the people in the parish were brilliant to work with, so it was a very positive experience.'

Between Quakerism and Roman Catholicism

Rachel loved the Catholic liturgy but there was no future there for her vocation to the priesthood. Her attitude to the priesthood is still markedly Quaker: 'I don't see ordination as some kind of privileged position above everybody else. The question of hierarchy is one objection Quakers would have to ordination. They would believe that everybody is there to minister to each other and to act as priests for each other, which is my position too.' The Catholic end of the Anglican Church seemed a good compromise so Rachel trained at an Anglo-Catholic theological college with a reputation for being strongly opposed to women's ordination! There were indeed tensions with those who claimed their opposition was a matter of conscience, conscience being very highly regarded among Quakers. 'You have to try to respect somebody else's issue of conscience while getting on and doing what you believe to be the right thing.'

Your busy day

Life in a parish is very hard work. 'It's really irritating when people say to you, "Oh, it's your busy day today, isn't it?" on a Sunday!

A typical day might include morning prayer at 7.45; dealing with post; taking a school assembly; taking communion to people at home; hospital visits; general visits in the parish, helping with all kinds of problems and crises; confirmation classes; lots of weddings, funerals and baptisms as well, not to mention meetings. We have a Eucharist almost every day and on Sunday about five services.' Rachel quite often gets asked to speak to groups such as the Mothers' Union or the Rotary Club. 'At the Rotary Club I talked about vocation and my work during the week. At other groups I often talk about life in Brazil – wealth and poverty and that kind of stuff – and people seem very interested. I'm also part of a committee at the moment which is trying to set up a drop-in centre for some of the teenagers who hang around outside church, quite often on freezing cold evenings, with nothing particular to do, too young to go into the pubs and too old to want to sit at home.'

No such thing as anonymity!

Rachel had found it difficult to get used to the loss of anonymity that comes with ordination. 'For example, when I was first ordained I joined the gym down at the local council-run sports centre and I was naïve enough to think it was possible to go there and just have a break away from everybody knowing who you were and what you did. But one time I was sitting there in the sauna and thinking I was perfectly anonymous when somebody very sweetly asked me how I was settling in at the church, so that just proved to me that there's no such thing as anonymity!

Gender stereotypes

'People are sometimes worried because they think that having a woman do something is going to be very different from having a man do something. You quite often hear the comment, "When I heard a woman was going to be doing the funeral I was really upset, but now we've met it's OK", and I think that's because they see that you're going to do things in a fairly standard way. Some people expect that women are going to do things in an untraditional way, or that they're going to be more kind and caring. People say things like, "Oh, you can talk to a woman much more easily than you can to a man." But that's just jumping straight into gender stereotypes. It's quite hard to see how you can be there in a positive way for somebody but without fulfilling all their gender stereotypes.'

Father? Or Mother? Or person?

Rachel felt that the question of women's distinctive contribution to the Church was exemplified by the question of what to call women who are ordained. 'At the Catholic end of the Church of England, in churches where it's customary to call a male priest Father, everybody wants to know what you're supposed to call a female priest. In some places it's argued that Father is a generic term and therefore you ought to call female priests Father as well. That seems a bit mad to me. The technical alternative to that is to call female priests Mother, implying the same role only exercised by different people. That might seem quite a good option except that placing the clergy in a parental position leaves the congregation in the position of being the priest's spiritual children and I'm not too sure whether the infantilization of the congregation is a healthy model to adopt! I think that if people could be seen just as people, and it could be recognized that everybody does ministry in different ways, then it could be a more healthy model of ministry than having one model for men and another model for women.'

LONGING TO SHOW SOLIDARITY – A MINISTER'S WIFE IN EL SALVADOR

We knew Baptist minister James Grote and his wife Susan because of their connection with El Salvador and thought it would be interesting to hear Susan's reflections on the two years they spent as missionaries in that country. They had first become aware of El Salvador when they saw a film of the assassination of Archbishop Oscar Romero in 1980, and of the shooting of mourners at his funeral. Salvadorean Baptist minister Marta Benavides had inspired them during her UK speaking tour shortly afterwards, and soon after James visited the country in 1988 they began preparing to be sent out by the Baptist Missionary Society. In August 1991 they departed, along with Daniel, nine, and Cameron, six, in spite of friends' misgivings about taking children to a country only just emerging from many years of civil war.

'We just want to be there'

Susan told us that when people asked them why they were going, what they were going to do, they answered, 'We're not going to do anything in particular, we just want to *be* there, standing alongside them.' But who were they to stand alongside, and how? 'At first', she recalled, 'nobody quite knew what to do with us, and I think that is true for many missionaries, everywhere.' They were sent to the large eastern town of San Miguel, the hottest town in the country, where heavy fighting during the war had made the Baptist ministers feel very isolated. 'They wanted us to be a kind of link between people there and the offices in the capital. We were attached to a small mission church linked to the main Baptist church in San Salvador and James was to travel round visiting and supporting the ministers.'

'Just a housewife'

Susan was somewhat tied to the home because the boys went to school at 7.30 and came home for lunch at 1.30, but being a housewife was a form of solidarity in itself. The boys played with local children and Susan found the neighbours very friendly and pleased to have an English family living alongside them (there were very few foreigners in the city). 'They were very good. Even silly things like big lizards running round the house – a neighbour would come in and slice the head off with a machete and think I was a bit funny not to want to kill it!'

But in Britain Susan is a pharmacist so she wanted to use her skills to help the community. 'The Baptist Association had a health education department so whenever they came to the east I went with them and we did basic hygiene talks about things like preventing cholera. I also did a little adult literacy work. But there were Salvadoreans there who were perfectly capable of doing that kind of thing, and without our language problems! It was frustrating that having got there, we weren't quite sure how to go about doing good.'

A straight up-and-down faith

The main trouble was that the Salvadorean Baptists, like most churches, were divided over what 'doing good' should mean. During the conflict there had been two camps: those, like Marta Benavides, for whom doing good meant struggling alongside the poor for social change, and those who had been taught to label that struggle 'communist subversion' and for whom doing good meant saving souls. 'The little mission church that we used to go to most Sundays was very closed-minded. You can understand why: they were in the worst conflict zone, they didn't want to be associated with it, they just didn't think about it, didn't want to talk about it, and didn't like it if we did. They were just there, a straight up-and-down faith, they didn't want to talk about Archbishop Romero or anything like that.' Nor did they approve of the other aspect of James' job which was to show round frequent foreign visitors who were keen to visit places like Ciudad Segundo Montes, the very well-organized community of returned refugees resettled north of San Miguel. 'We had a car with the Baptist Association logo on the side and people said, "We're always seeing your car going up to the guerrillas." It didn't go down well.'

The crunch came

When the Grotes returned to San Miguel after a Christmas break in 1993 a huge split between 'left' and 'right' had occurred among the Baptists and they found themselves ostracized by most of the local churches. 'We tried to remain neutral, never pushed our own opinions and just tried to be pastoral and help in whatever small ways we could. But I became more concerned about the boys because after the war ended common crime mushroomed and although our budget was modest we were perceived as having pots of money compared to most Salvadoreans and that made us an obvious target. The last straw was when James was kidnapped on a trip when he could easily have had Cameron with him. He was unharmed but they took the car. So in March 1994 we left in a hurry and were glad to get away, which was sad.' Thus they indeed found themselves standing alongside the countless Salvadoreans persecuted or exiled for what we certainly think of as 'doing good'.

A reverse culture shock

Back in England, Susan said, the two boys 'found school a bit of a doddle. They'd been used to a very strict regime: classes of about 50 and just copying from a blackboard all the time. Sitting round tables and chatting they found quite astonishing. For us a new phenomenon was stopping at traffic lights and having someone try to sell us roses or wipe our windscreen. We'd lived with that kind of thing in El Salvador, where the homeless people in the streets were really desperate, so we automatically bought some roses and gave the guy some money for the cleaning. Other people in the car would say, 'What are you doing? Just say No. Those people are making a packet.' Such different attitudes to the same situation. And the way everybody over there greets you as you walk by – nobody even catches your eye in this country.'

The very different journeys of these women have one thing in common: they are journeys undertaken in faithful response to a call, and in courageous readiness to encounter the new, even to experience a culture shock in reverse!

~ 8 ~

Helping Urban Churches to Respond

Jenny Richardson has been National Co-ordinator of UNLOCK (formerly Evangelical Urban Training Project, EUTP) for eight years, and has now been given Chief Executive responsibility. We heard about her and her work from Chris Rowland, Dean Ireland Professor of the Exegesis of Holy Scripture at Oxford University, who is also on the Management Group of the British Liberation Theology Project.

'This isn't fair . . .'

Jenny was brought up a nominal Anglican with a very working-class background. Because she passed the 11-plus she made it through the education system and got to university, where she found her own faith. 'One of my first recollections of justice issues,' she said, 'was when I was part of the student action group and used to take a party of Asian children from the St Paul's area for days out on Saturdays. At that time I went to a very nice, very lively Anglican church in Bristol with all the students. The families there were so nice to us, we'd go round for Sunday lunch, so that one day I was with these poor Asian kids from St Paul's, and the next with these white middle-class kids in Bristol who were part of the church. And I thought there was something wrong in this somewhere. The Asian ones hadn't even got what is considered "the right religion", they'd got nothing. I wouldn't have given it the name "justice issues" at that point. I just thought, "This isn't fair, it isn't right", and that stayed with me.'

Jenny went on to train as a youth worker. 'I was in London for a while, then moved up to a Christian community in North Yorkshire, but I'd always got this hankering feeling about the inner city and coming back to the urban, and to my own working-class roots. I came to Sheffield, and for a variety of reasons committed myself to this local church, St John's, quite near the city centre. I lived first of all with a family from the church, and then after 18 months I got a flat in Hyde Park flats as they then were, a big high-rise block, seventh floor up. While I was there I met Geoff whom I'm now married to. He was a student also living in the flats, also committed to the area. I suppose I came in with this naïve attitude that as an individual Christian I could actually make a difference to this place. I think I left saying, "There's got to be structural change!" It was living there that did it, and particularly living there until Matthew our eldest was just over a year old. Living in it as a single person, going out to work and coming back, was all right. But living on the seventh floor, with lifts not working, with milk-men refusing to deliver, with washing-machine repairers refusing to come, with people spraying for ants all over the baby's nappies, all this sort of thing, I thought "This just isn't on". It changed my whole attitude.

'Jesus was human . . .'

'We ran a house group there and we had all sorts of folks who wouldn't have come to the main house groups. I kept thinking this house group was going to fold because people kept moving out of the flats, but we always seemed to find other people that would come. I can remember doing this Bible study with a group of people, looking at the fact that Jesus was human, and this single Mum, with a look of horror on her face, just said, "Mary didn't have disposable nappies, did she?" She was suddenly seeing Jesus as a real baby, and his Mum didn't have disposable nappies, and it would have been a real pain in the neck for Mary, because she'd have had all the mucky nappies. And suddenly seeing a light dawn for this woman was really amazing. We lived there until the flats were going to be demolished and we moved out.

Reflecting on what had happened

'We decided that we needed to do something else for other people who were still in the flats, left behind when most people were moving out, so we ran this sort of café on a Saturday lunchtime in the Community Centre. It only lasted a few months but I think for this little group it was quite a powerful experience. We'd got all sorts of characters: there was one chap who was a down-and-out who hung around the market – he always used to wash the baked potatoes, so at least his hands saw water! Another man only had one arm, and he felt he couldn't do anything. So we asked "Will you help us do teas? You can hold a teapot." So he ended up doing the teas with his one arm, feeling "Oh, I can do this."

'We had house group sessions then. Looking back, I think it was doing theology from experience, but I wouldn't have seen it like that then. I just did it because it worked, and I think, looking back on it, I'm glad I've done it that way round. We would use the house groups to reflect on what had happened. So the week everybody had had a row because somebody didn't turn up on time with the key, and somebody else was narked about it, we actually did a group session on forgiveness. All sorts of people were moving home, so we did a Bible study on "What's our attitude to our home?" It was very interesting. "Welcome strangers into your home", but if you live in these flats you daren't, all of those sorts of questions, very interesting. We closed the house group two days before Sam was born, there wasn't anybody else to take it on. Geoff was working shift work, I tried carrying on with Matthew toddling about but it reached a point where there wasn't anybody else we could pass it on to. It was a very sad moment, but I thought, "I just can't do this, I'm about to have a baby, I can't be responsible for running this house group."'

With the new baby, they moved to their present house and while the children were little Jenny worked with trainees and staff of the Youth Training Scheme. Then, after a few years as a northern net-worker for the Evangelical Coalition for Mission she became national worker with UNLOCK. Jenny feels that the UNLOCK work runs parallel to her home life, and both feed each other so it didn't matter that it was half-term and we were meeting in her home rather than her office – 'Being here is as important as what I do there.'

'What the heck are we doing here?'

The family had to move out of the house temporarily last summer – 'This bay window was collapsing, then they found the front wall wasn't ever pinned to the rest of the house either!' – and when they moved back Jenny felt she needed to take some time out to work out a fresh vision of all that was happening in her life. 'At times we think, "What the heck are we doing here? Why are we here with local kids throwing stones at the windows, our car consistently vandalized, what on earth do we think we're doing?" I was also getting more and more frustrated with our local church, feeling less and less at home with institutional forms of being a church. I was about to start the research for this MA on adult education with theological reflection, particularly looking at the education of radical theological educators – how do you train them to be educators? There was the fact of living here, and there was the fact that EUTP was changing its name to UNLOCK – what was the new vision for that organization? I thought these strands were connected but I didn't know how. I needed some space, and with the family around and all the responsibilities there, I couldn't come home and say, "This is my space, I can do what I want to do" because I'd be sorting out the Lego bricks or the fights or the washing, or all the family things. So I took a three-month gap from church, which felt very naughty, but I did, and I used the time for questioning: "What am I supposed to be doing here?" and about UNLOCK and about the MA, and the question became "What does it mean to be church here, in this street? What does it actually mean here, with all the things that go on?" The conclusion I came to was that asking the question was what it meant to be church, so being church meant continuing to say, "What does it mean to be church, here, now?" I worked it out for myself here, and then I found it paralleled in a book of liberation theology by Gustavo Gutiérrez! I thought, Yes!'

'The stable was mucky . . .'

Jenny is responsible for finding and training volunteers to be radical theological educators in their own areas. 'What we want from these trainers is for them to be people who are also asking that question and who will stand with those who are struggling with the question. Not the people who have got all the answers but those who will stand and work it through where they are. The MA was about "How do you train people to do that task?" So it felt as if the whole thing was dropping into place. That's probably where I'm at at the moment.

'We were talking earlier on about theology from the bottom, and I suppose that's what I've tried to do but haven't realized that that's what I was doing. I can remember one Christmas when the kids were quite small, and I was standing at the school gates. I was just like everybody else, it was Christmas and you're supposed to clean the paint-work and tidy everywhere up and rush around like a demented idiot, trying to make Christmas as it's supposed to look and be. And then I thought, "This is absolutely stupid". There were loads of other women in the same state as me, "I haven't done this, I haven't done that", and I just kept on saying "The stable was mucky" and you could just see the relief on their faces, that they hadn't actually got to go about cleaning up, because the stable was mucky.

Seeing the Bible from a different perspective

'You start to see different things in the Bible once people have taken it from their own perspective. We occasionally try to have a proper family meal, in the midst of the rush of life. One Saturday a couple of years ago, we'd been shopping and then we had this meal together, and Matthew had finished his tea – we'd had tuna pizza – and he said he would find something to read from the Bible. He came back with the story of the feeding of the 5000, because, he said, "Well, it's about food isn't it? We've just all been shopping in Safeways and now we're having tea here, so it's all about food." He looked at the passage and he said, "The disciples shared the food out, didn't they?"

'And then this lad came round – he lived a few doors down – and he'd obviously not had his tea, and he was a bit embarrassed. To ask him to sit at the table would have been too threatening, but Matthew went out to play with him, and then came back in and took the last piece of tuna pizza and just said "The disciples shared bread and fish. So am I," and just took it out and gave it to this lad. And you think, Yes, this boy has actually learned that you do it locally and real, and it wasn't, "Oh, it's really about a miracle, about Jesus." He had said "This is about me doing the thing that the disciples did."

'What I find interesting is being told we've got it wrong, sometimes! One of UNLOCK's people in Hull did a Bible study for another organization. It was the bit about James and John wanting the best place, next to Jesus, and she did the Bible study based on the fact that everybody was of value, everybody was important, and she was told, "No, that isn't what the passage is about, it's about not trying to get the first place." And she said, "Not if you're one of the ones that are stood on, it's not." So when you actually start to see the Bible from a different perspective, you're told, "You've got this wrong."

The Full Monty

'The thing we're most notorious for is a Bible study based on *The Full Monty*. It just seemed like life as we know it, ordinary blokes from around Sheffield, who had everything stacked against them, and survived. We used it to get people to tell their own stories, and then we linked them into the Bible. When I was doing it just over a year ago, I remember sitting in the Good Friday service and thinking: "Goodness, I have now got a new understanding of what it might have meant to Jesus to be stripped of his garments" – and then thinking, "You're not supposed to think that!" But having actually watched the film and seen the vulnerability of people, you just thought, "Yes, there's a new insight here." And Geoff said, "You can't put that in the pack! Don't put that in the pack!" He was really worried. This pack has gone all over the show, even into prisons. What did surprise us was the very nice ladies in Tunbridge Wells who used it and said, "You know, we talk to each other now." The place that wouldn't use it was an academic institution. There was an administrator there who'd seen it around and bought it and tried to get the college staff to use it, and they'd just laughed, "You can't do a Bible study on that." Which to me meant that they were laughing at where I live. "You can't do Bible study round here" is what they're telling me.

'A struggle just being a wife . . .'

'But being here, being a Mum, actually gives weight to what I'm doing. My two roles feed each other. I've been in a number of situations where people who were talking about urban mission don't live there and don't come across the hassle of it day to day. I don't think we fully come across it – there are worse things happening and more difficult areas than this – but I do think that living here with the kids we're forced to face up to some of the stuff that's around. It's been a struggle just being a wife as well. When I first got married and I was living in the flats, somebody sent me a book on how to be a good Christian wife. It had a picture on the front of the doily for the biscuits and this sort of thing, but the phrase that stuck with me was: "You can tell a woman's attitude to God by the way she keeps her house!" Some of the images that get put across of how women are supposed to be just do not fit. *I've* got the out and about ministry job in this family, and people ask my husband, "How do you manage for your dinner, Geoff?" ("Well, I cook it"). Geoff has actually chosen not to go for promotion at work because it would tie him down too much (he's the homeless officer with the council), but that means that other people can cover him and he can get the time off to cover the family if I need to be out and about. I work for a small organization with limited funding. I'm not paid particularly well for the out and about job which takes an awful lot of time, so you're trying to juggle the family end, and make ends meet, and all that sort of thing, at the same time. But at least we know what it feels like. We do go to the market to shop, which is where you meet lots of the local people – I love the market. But being a Mum – it's like the root of what we're doing, it gives me credibility to do the other job and to speak out, because I know I'm quite a theoretical person naturally, but I actually talk here from my guts, because I know how life is here, so it's both ends of the spectrum. I'm getting more and more opportunities to speak, and I think some of it is because of this combination of roles.

The story of UNLOCK

'UNLOCK started life,' Jenny told us, 'as the Evangelical Urban Training Project, about 27 years ago, out of concern that urban people were not given opportunities to have their say; their way of expressing faith wasn't affirmed; the Church was middle-class and most of the education in the Church is very middle-class and academic. So a package was developed to use with urban work-shops around the country, to get local people to tell their stories, looking at their church, their area, their faith. Some of it is still being used. It was very much local people doing it for themselves. And then the money ran out. It's been a very hand-to-mouth exis-tence. Now a main source of funding is a sponsored walk once a year when we organize a big walk through Central London some-where, using local inner-city churches as check points, a different route each year. We've got a lot of support from Essex and Surrey and Hampshire, people from the big wealthy churches all come to the walk and get sponsored, and that keeps us going for another year.'

When they ran out of money they thought it would be a cheaper option to have somebody half-time to train local people, local trainers, to do the job, rather than doing it all themselves: 'I've got work experience of training trainers, so the job has been a meshing of that style of professional training, plus my urban mission experience. I came into it about seven years ago and we've struggled on. I was keen to develop teams rather than individuals in places, and we've got some very interesting things going on. We've got a little group in the Midlands who are trying to put together a pack based on Romans. The vicars keep saying, "We need to get some doctrine – let's sort out Romans, how to do Romans with urban people." So they're doing that. There's a very creative group in Hull using a lot of art – for example, at one workshop they put a curtain across the sanctuary to represent the barriers between people and the church, and they ripped that down and had fish and chips in the sanctuary, the banquet in God's presence! There's a little group, a couple of people in Sheffield and Rotherham now, there's a group emerging in Leeds, there's a little group in London. This way of doing things, with group work rather than it all coming from the top, and people expressing their own opinions, is very different from what it was like 25 years ago. There's much more openness to participative learning now, with people working at regional and diocesan level.

UNLOCK – unlocking the real life stories of people

'About the name change – for a long time we've not been comfortable with EUTP. It was set up in its day as the right name for its time, and it is still helpful for the evangelical churches to be challenged by it, because often the evangelical churches will have quite a narrow view of what their mission is, and they need to be encouraged into community involvement which is one of the things we do. But it's been such a pain in the neck when you go anywhere. You would say, "I'm from the Evangelical Urban Training Project – but we're not what you think we are!" We felt we had to unpack all the images people had of what "evangelical" meant. We are "urban", and that is our focus – but this method is relevant for everybody, it isn't just a case of "Oh well, these people haven't made it at school, so we'll give them a nice easy method." It is actually relevant theology, theological methodology for everybody, so "urban" is a bit questionable. "Training"? That sounds like top down training, and actually we're about education from the bottom up, so training isn't quite the right word, and "project" sounds like here today, gone tomorrow, and we're here for keeps. So all in all it wasn't a good name.

'We spent ages trying to work out what it should be. We started with a mission statement. It took about 18 months, but in the end we got a mission statement that makes sense, because in it there is so much about educational and theological method.

UNLOCK
Unlocking real life stories of urban people
Revealing good news of the down-to-earth Christ
Releasing life-changing skills and confidence

It's about unlocking real life stories to start with, and then looking at the Bible. It's about releasing skills and confidence, it isn't about knowledge, so that seemed to be the right balance, really positive. And then when you look at the middle bits, the theology is all there as well. In "good news of the down-to-earth Christ" you've got revelation, you've got incarnation, but it doesn't say who is doing the revealing. The normal way it is received, through the priest or church leader, is not there. People could read it there if they choose to, but actually the good news is revealed through the unlocking of the story, and "down-to-earth Christ" seemed to be a phrase that summed up the incarnation: Jesus as one of us. We also had an interesting debate about the logo. Even that took a long time to get. Somebody wanted the cross on the circular bit of the key but we chose to put it in the city skyline. Christ had to be in the city, not outside looking in, but actually here, in the city. So even the logo, the image, says something. UNLOCK has a struggle to survive, and we've got potential to develop all over the place. People are asking for us, and we just end up running round in circles trying to meet the needs that are there.

Learning from the urban church

'I feel that the point is coming when the urban church has a lot to teach the rest of the Church, but we haven't got the resources to do it. We've got tied up in knots in groups when we've been trying to define what we mean by urban! When I write something for my assignments I always put "those who are without power and choice and marginalized in an urban context" or something like that. I'm talking about the people at the bottom who are getting pushed around by other people. That's where my heart is – among people who get pushed around and get treated as if they're not important, and the Church treats the urban church in the same way. We're being made to jump through hoops about mission and all sorts of things, so we can pay our way. We've now had to share a vicar with another church. We used to have three members of staff, it's a huge parish. Sheffield diocese has got to lose 25 clergy over five years. I might be wrong but it seems as if they're going to be putting the squeeze on some of the poorer churches, because we're not paying our way. Is that right? Haven't we got enough to be doing without that? One of the things that appals me is, in our church at the moment, one of the people who actually makes incredible efforts to keep friends who are not part of the church, will have people round for meals, just to be mates with people, runs the cricket club which draws in all sorts of people in the church and on the edge of it – because of the lack of clergy has found himself doing a lot of the running round organizing the church, and you just think, What a waste! It does feel as if the needs of the urban church are not addressed by the wider Church. Things like the Alpha course. They've got a big poster advertising "Life is not just nine to five" – well, people round here don't get jobs, and if they do it's probably shift work, so it's an insult. I'm getting cross, and I can feel it! It seems as if the wider Church does not see what life is like round here, and they put expectations on people, and people believe it, people round here feel, "We ought to be a church like them over there." They shouldn't be. They've got so much, *they're* the wider Church.'

The key question for Jenny, 'What does it mean to be church here and now?' is perhaps the key question for the churches at the beginning of this third millennium. 'The good news is revealed through the unlocking of the stories', she tells us. Jenny's own story is good news for women struggling with the competing commitments to family life and to 'those without power and choice and marginalized'. Her conviction, born of the experience of living life from the perspective of the Bible, that each commitment feeds on the other, is immensely encouraging and liberating.

ザ

9

Seeking Richer Spiritual Food

Bernadette Askins invited us to a meeting of the Catholic Women's Network in Newcastle. We accordingly travelled up there and were met by Bernadette, who took us to the home of Pat Sumpter where the meeting was to take place. Over a restorative cup of tea round the kitchen table, where Jo Forster and Frances Blodwell joined us, Bernadette and Pat gave us a little background information.

The Catholic Women's Network started in the early 1980s: the catalyst for a group of women in the North East had been a weekend conference at the Catholic seminary Upholland in Skelmersdale, 'Women in the Church'. For Bernadette this conference was 'a complete eye-opener. It made explicit a lot of things I'd been thinking about or pondering on over the years. At the end of the conference we decided that we wouldn't let things drop, we'd all keep in touch, and we began to meet here in the North East. We began with about four women, and it rapidly grew to about ten.' Another group, calling itself the Catholic Women's Network, had started meeting in London, and from these two groups the Network spread out into different parts of the country, eventually totalling about 500 members.

Untraditional spirituality

The general aim of the Network is to offer support to those who do not feel at home in the traditional church framework, and a spirituality which does not depend on the traditional forms. Membership was not exclusively Roman Catholic – there were Anglicans and Methodists, and a Muslim woman regularly attended the meetings. They came to the Network, Pat told us,

124

because 'they were dissatisfied with their church setting, then met somebody who was a Network member who said, "Look, I think you might find a little support on a Friday night at our meeting." That's how I came to it. But there are very small numbers of such women in parishes. I have to say that awareness-raising, even in terms of inclusive language, has been unsuccessful.'

Bernadette added, 'There will be those who are still in contact with parish life and who regard the meeting of the Network as a way of finding the kind of support they wouldn't normally find for the kind of issues we discuss. Then there would be those hanging on to parish life and going to meetings of the CWN occasionally. There are also a number of people in the Network who have left the Catholic Church: they've found it so painful and demoralizing and having gone through a period of agonizing have finally left. They haven't joined another Church, but they continue to come to this group.'

Although the original purpose of the Network was to provide a meeting space for women who were searching for another way of being church, this inevitably leads to action, such as the support the Network gave to Anglican women during their campaign for the ordination of women, joining them at prayer and attending some of their rallies, including the final one at Coventry. 'We had a lot of Anglican members who were going to be ordained priests in their Church. They came to Catholic Women's Network meet-ings regularly and found a great deal of support. Members of Catholic Women's Network were outside Durham Cathedral on the morning of their ordination, carrying banners and balloons. When people saw them, they said, "Well, it'll be you next." Sadly, once they were ordained and got parishes things changed and most of the Anglican women no longer had time to attend regularly.

Women playing an active part

'We have a huge shortage of clergy in our diocese of Hexham and Newcastle,' said Bernadette. 'Lay people, women in particular, are playing a very much more active role at ground level, and now we are beginning to find appointments being made at regional level. Recently our diocese has appointed women into significant posts.

My appointment as Diocesan Ecumenical Officer, in 1997, is one. Other women have been appointed as Financial Secretary and Adult Religious Education Advisor. A woman is secretary of the Diocesan Pastoral Council and Council of Laity. But it's a slow process. When I went to speak to the Council of Priests, it was me and 60 men. The decision-making is still with the Bishop and the Council of Priests, though the Council of Laity are being consulted more.'

Sadly, the question is how much the people in the pews want things to change. 'As you scratch the surface,' Pat said, 'you find that those who are left in the pews are not actually yearning for great changes. And that's what's frightening.'

Meeting new challenges

'One of the problems', Bernadette feels, 'is that there is no realization that things are going to be changing all the time as both the Church and society come up against new challenges. There hasn't been sufficient ongoing education for priests and people to help them to adjust and plan ahead. One new factor is the changing role of women and our expectations. We no longer expect to be invisible in church. We want to see our experience and insights valued and to be fully involved in making decisions. Women are leaving the Church and not staying to see changes happen. They get upset and frustrated with the situation.'

There was another factor to be taken into account, Bernadette said. 'The large numbers of women who are bringing up children and have time to spare to get involved in church life just don't exist any more. Most women with young children are now working part- or full-time. The younger group of women has gone, and what you have instead is groups like ours, who are retiring earlier. You see a lot of women who are retired or semi-retired and are playing a large part in actually running the church at local level. A major change that has been predicted is towards running parishes with a team made up of a priest and a lay leader. A number of women are doing theology degrees, and they might well in future be running a parish with a priest, since at present one priest often looks after two parishes.'

Diocesan Ecumenical Officer

Bernadette represents the diocese of Hexham and Newcastle at meetings where ecumenical work is on the agenda. She works with the Catholic community, attending Pastoral Area Councils and Parish Councils, talking about good practice and giving examples of how the churches could be working together on the ground. Some areas, like sacramental sharing of the Eucharist, are difficult, others like social justice and community action offer excellent opportunities for working together. Bernadette organizes meetings in North East England for people across the denominations who are responsible for certain aspects, like justice and peace, social responsibility, or the third world. The hope is to co-ordinate efforts and share resources.

The Decade of Churches in Solidarity with Women – 1988 to 1998

Women in the North East were active throughout the Decade, one of the aims of which was to make visible the contribution of women to the churches. The North East Ecumenical Women's Group invited women's organizations from all the churches to contribute squares to a huge quilt, each square to celebrate the life of a Christian woman. When finished, 72 women were portrayed in embroidery or appliqué, some of them very local, all of them women who in one way or another had made a difference to society. Mrs Helen Bott, a vicar's wife from Stockton, for instance, rode round on a penny-farthing bicycle doing good works; Josephine Butler, from Morpeth, allied herself with women who were not only poor but who were moral outcasts because they were prostitutes. She led a successful campaign in the nineteenth century against the Contagious Diseases Acts which deprived them of their constitutional rights in law. Alison Kay at the age of 80 started a friendship kitchen under the arches of the bridge in Newcastle where homeless and lonely people could come for a meal.

The end of the Decade was marked in the UK by a conference in Durham, 'Forward to the Promised Community', and a celebration in Durham Cathedral at Easter 1998. The official ending of the Decade was a World Council of Churches celebration in

Harare in November. The Durham celebration gave the 1400 women who took part in it a feeling that they had literally crossed over a line of demarcation. 'The liturgy was in inclusive language,' Frances said, 'and it was wonderful to feel the cathedral was ours and we belonged there. There's a line at the back of the cathedral across which women were not supposed to tread, but on that day it was our place, it wasn't just a place we were allowed in on sufferance.' The quilt was displayed there for the first time.

Bernadette felt that there had been many positive results of the Decade. 'The national churches had all begun to look at ways to ensure women had a voice and some had taken practical action to try to make this happen. The Catholic Church had set up a joint dialogue between women and the bishops to discuss issues and concerns. However, generally it was very apparent to the women that this had been a decade of women in solidarity with women, and a decade of women in solidarity with the churches, but not always of churches in solidarity with women! There was a feeling that there was still quite a lot of work to be done.' Kathy Galloway of the Iona Community had commented that the closing of the Decade was 'not the end of the work, but just the beginning; full participation in the life of the Church is still only a dream for millions of women.'

Sharing nourishment

The CWN meeting proper began with a buffet supper, to which the ten or 12 members present had contributed, and continued with a liturgy, most imaginatively prepared, which included a reading from *Life out of Death: The Feminine Spirit in El Salvador* – women speaking to women across cultures. Newspaper cuttings highlighting current local and national issues were put out and people were invited to choose one, reflect on it, and respond by placing in the centre a paper flame for anger, a teardrop for sorrow, or a heart for forgiveness. The liturgy ended with a prayer, and was followed by a discussion of local and national issues – the place of women in society, for example, and the difficulties which arise for women who try to combine a career with motherhood. It was clear that being able to voice doubts and share problems in an understanding and accepting atmosphere was a supportive and strengthening experience for this diverse group of women.

(We also joined a small, ecumenical group of women in Oxford in one of the monthly meetings which they too find enriching for their spiritual life, and we get the impression there are many similar informal groups coming together all over the country.)

THE CATHOLIC WOMEN'S NETWORK IN YORK
(CATHOLIC DIOCESE OF MIDDLESBROUGH)

From Newcastle we travelled to York for conversations with CWN women prominent in the churches, and a meeting with justice and peace activists. We were met at the station by Nan Saeki, who had put us in touch with the CWN women, and who was our hostess for two nights. Nan is outstandingly public-spirited: her many activities include Chair of the National Liaison Committee of Diocesan Justice and Peace groups (now the National Justice and Peace Network) for four years from 1993, Chair of the Middlesbrough Diocesan Justice and Peace Commission for five years, until 1996 (she is now the Treasurer), and a founder member of the Diocesan Women's Commission, of which Pamela Ellis is the Chair. Nan had arranged for us to do an interview with BBC Radio York that evening ('Why are you here?', 'What is the point of the conversations?', 'Why just women?', 'Do you hope for anything constructive to come out of this?' – all questions which gave us an opportunity to talk about the women we had met and the importance of hearing their voices and bringing them to visibility).

The next morning saw us at the Pastoral Centre next door to the Bar Convent for an early start. Pamela Ellis was the first of the women we spoke to. Pamela had attended a convent day school in the pre-Vatican II era; Vatican II with its hopeful promise of change coincided with her teenage years, she remembered the first Mass in English during her first year at Manchester University and the new sense of participation in the liturgy in the lively and supportive Catholic chaplaincy.

'Something missing'

After the exciting, Vatican II-inspired Catholic life at university, ordinary parish life was a shock with its anonymity and lack of welcome, and Pamela began to drift away from the Church, a process accelerated by her marriage to someone who didn't share her faith. The Mass began to drop out of her life, even though this left her with a feeling of 'something missing'. For a time the 'something missing' was filled by a personal experience of God through the charismatic renewal movement, but after a few years when that movement began drifting to the right, Pamela couldn't follow it. That left another gap, which gradually came to be filled by an increasing interest in women's experience in general and women's spirituality in particular (helped by the women's support group which she and a few friends started in the early 90s).

The Gospels through the eyes of a woman

This phase in her life, Pamela told us, was enriched by an experience of The Spiritual Exercises of St Ignatius Loyola (a programme for those making a retreat with the object of finding God's will for their lives, which uses Gospel texts as passages for meditation). 'This led me to think about the Gospels in new ways, looking at them through the lens of my experience of being a woman. For instance, it struck me that the language of breaking, bleeding, giving oneself, which is used at the Last Supper, is also the language of childbirth. Insights like this drew me into thinking and writing about the way women approach the Gospels, and into studying theology at MA level – initially as a way of becoming more credible as a writer, but soon for its own sake.'

In the course of her studies at the College of Ripon and York St John, Pamela wrote assignments on feminist theology, suffering (a theological reflection on the death in a car crash of a whole family of her friends), Mary Ward (foundress of the Institute of the Blessed Virgin Mary), and suicide (a study of traditional Christian, secular Western, and Japanese attitudes, and a 'new' theology of suicide based on the concept of the body of Christ, and how a community which genuinely valued each individual while also being a supportive network might eliminate one of the major causes of suicide, loneliness).

Middlesbrough Diocesan Women's Commission

When Bishop John Crowley of Middlesbrough decided in the summer of 1997 to set up a Diocesan Women's Commission (the first diocese to do so), Pamela was persuaded to put her name forward as a possible chairperson, and was appointed. The inaugural meeting in York in January 1998 was followed by others in different parts of the diocese, the initial aim being to get to know people and build up relationships and trust.

Doing visible things

'Now I feel we are beginning to move into actually doing things. We are building up a register of women with their qualifications and experience; this will say to the diocese, "Look, this is an amazing resource – here are all these women with all these gifts and talents and professional expertise, ready to make a contribution." We can only hope that some use may be made of it.'

The Commission is also setting up a working party to see whether women have specific ways of working which are different from men's ways and could complement them. 'So we're beginning to move into doing visible things which the diocese can actually see.'

Overcoming suspicion

A former mayor of Hull wrote her appreciation of the Women's Commission in a letter to Pamela Ellis which was published in the newsletter. Her comments succinctly condense the feelings of many women in the churches: 'I have long felt the need for more participation by women in church affairs, and not just tea-making either.' And 'Believe me dear, it won't be easy. I know only too well. We are not always welcome in the male domain!'

Pamela saw that the inclusion of women in planning and decision-making would be a gradual process. 'There's a lot of residual suspicion, not just on the part of the clergy but also on the part of a lot of women. "Who are these people? Do they think they're speaking for us?" To have rushed in would have alienated more people than it would have won over. I think it's very important to bring as many people as possible along with us.' For this, a process of education would be necessary. 'That's another reason why we felt we had to go fairly slowly at first, because all of us in the core group have been involved in women's issues and thought about them for years, and we tend to assume that everybody has reached the same point, but they haven't! You've got to start where the majority of people are and build on that.'

The feminine approach

It was important, too, to be a non-threatening presence to the clergy as well as to other women. Bishop John Crowley would be very supportive – he set up the Commission – but the clergy would be at different stages along the line. 'They've always been invited to our meetings. One priest did come to a meeting, and it was quite interesting, he had a different style, he brought a very masculine style into what was essentially a women's meeting, and it was very odd. He was very definite and dogmatic and interrupted people; he wasn't being antagonistic, it was just a different style. But it was an interesting experience. Women try to be conciliatory, on the whole, and try to bring in everybody's point of view.'

At the end of our conversation, to Marigold's question 'What do you feel that you'd most like to write about?', Pamela answered, 'I would like to go on writing about the women's angle. What I feel I do best is looking at the Gospel through women's eyes. That's where my heart is.'

Work with people on the margins

Pat O'Connor's heart is in working for children with disabilities, but she is also a member of the Middlesbrough Diocesan Women's Commission, of which Pamela Ellis is the Chair; and is the Diocese's link with the National Board of Catholic Women, on which she represents CWN.

We were talking about the recent book edited by Paul Vallely, *The New Politics: Catholic Social Teaching for the 21st Century* (SCM Press, 1998), and Pat commented that out of seven contributors, only one was a woman. 'I'm sure that it never occurred to the editor that all the commentaries but one arise out of men's experience. It's an attitude that is institutionalized in the Church.' Like Pamela Ellis, Pat recognizes that the process of breaking down suspicion and introducing changes would have to involve men *and* women. 'It just doesn't occur to the clergy, most of the time, that they're not including women in their thinking, and if you point out where inclusive language could have been used in the liturgy, they say, "Oh, it didn't occur to me. I didn't notice." They don't mean anything by it. A lot of women don't recognize sexist language either. They say, "What are you making all the fuss about?" So a big job of education has to be done.'

It will be a gradual process. 'It's about working with priests who are sympathetic and more enlightened, and about gently suggesting – threatening people doesn't work – to the others that a different translation might be useful. Our bishop, John Crowley, is very sensitive to language, and so if he approves of a suggestion we are able to go along to the priests with it and say, "Well, the bishop uses it!", so that's quite helpful. Language reflects attitudes.'

Far from reality

Pat felt there was a lack of understanding of how change happens. 'It may come from the top down, but it's mostly from the grass-roots upwards. I think this has caused a major problem in the Church in Western Europe: the lives of women here are so far removed from what the Vatican is telling us to do or not to do that it's become almost an irrelevance. Contraception, the question of divorced and remarried people in the Eucharist, all these sorts of issues are very far removed from the reality of people's lives. I don't think contraception is an issue for the young generation – they just use it. We had our first child just at the time of *Humanae Vitae* [Pope Paul VI's 1968 encyclical banning contraception] and everybody expected a change. When *Humanae Vitae* came out and there was obviously no significant change, it was a watershed, I think: people then began obeying their conscience, not just in that area but in all areas of their faith. Our first child has severe learning difficulties; lots of people have children with genetic factors, meaning they would always have a child with a disability, so what are they to do in their married life? These issues just aren't taken on board by the Vatican. And of course they're not taken on board by a lot of priests either.'

In touch with people's problems

Pat didn't work when her children were small, but she trained and qualified as a social worker in 1993. After five years in child care she got a job in a special team for children with disabilities. 'That's where my heart was. It raises lots of issues. We have to deal with situations where babies are very ill from birth, either they've been born with a life-threatening or life-limiting condition, or they've contracted one at birth. So we have to put families through that very painful decision: whether they allow their children to die, switch off ventilators. Yesterday, for instance, we got a referral from a health colleague in the hospital where a 16-year-old mother, who already had an 18-month-old child, had had a baby. He got meningitis when he was a day old, and it's left him with massive brain damage, so we've been asked to look at what support we can give once the baby comes out of hospital.

'I've got somebody else at the moment whose little girl has got cystic fibrosis, she's 19 now, and the child is three. She's also got a baby of four months who's OK. Her partner is 17 but is acting emotionally like a 14-year-old, so they keep splitting up and getting back together, but they just fight with each other. It's not an oppression of the woman, they just fight like a couple of 14-year-olds would do. That's OK except that they've got the two children, and the one with cystic fibrosis needs constant attention, and physiotherapy and medication and so on.'

A spiritual foundation

In answer to our question whether the people Pat met had any spiritual beliefs, she said that in her experience people do not have a strong faith to help them deal with their problems. 'Our area has quite a high Catholic population, but I would say that people probably have a belief in God but don't practise their faith. Social work is an interesting profession, certainly in our area, because it's got a high proportion of people who've got a Roman Catholic background, though they may not practise. All three of us in my team have got Roman Catholic backgrounds. If you know that somebody has a faith background, Catholic or Anglican or Methodist or whatever, it's quite a useful way of connecting with them and helping in difficult situations: you can talk about the strength they can get from their faith, which you wouldn't normally do in a social work context. You would need to be very sensitive and know quite a bit about the individual before you use those sorts of opportunities.'

A deprived community

Pat's office is based in Stockton, which like other areas in the North is suffering from the loss of its industrial base. 'People are being made redundant, so you have areas of intense deprivation, and you have areas like the one where our office is based, which is quite middle-class. One of the estates in Stockton was raided by the police last weekend: they were looking for drugs, and they arrested quite a lot of people. But the consequence of that was that our child placement team were left with 14 children to accommodate on Friday, the day before the weekend, because their parents had been arrested and remanded in custody. Fortunately they managed to place most of them with relatives at the end of the day, and we only had to place four with foster parents. The knock-on effect on all levels is quite significant. Something like 80% of men on that estate don't have jobs. And the problem is that the local authorities rehouse people who've already got problems, with other people who've got problems, so of course it gets difficult. People's spirits are just totally crushed, hopeless, because of the grind of living on Income Support year after year after year – you're up to third-generation families who've never had jobs. People daren't go out at night. It's dreadful.'

No more jobs-for-life

The jobs on offer in the area are often very low-paid, part-time jobs. Pat's husband had been unemployed for a few years and it had been a dreadful experience, although they had an infrastructure of house, car and clothes so that their situation was not as stark as that of the people on the estates, who had neither the material backing nor the support of people better off than they were.

Pat's faith is very important to her. 'My spirituality comes from my background with the Marist Fathers. It goes beautifully with social work, because one of its facets is the divine mercy, work with people on the margins, including people in the church – it all fits in.'

The Catholic Women's Network and a justice and peace group recently set up in the parish keep Pat in touch with national and international issues, and membership of a Christian Life Community group gives her a local support base at which to refuel her extremely demanding commitments to making things better for others. 'It's mostly Roman Catholic, but not exclusively. They are like Base Christian Communities. We think that's definitely where the future of the Church is, in small groups.'

SUPPORT FOR YOUR SPIRITUAL JOURNEY

Woodbrooke Quaker Study Centre in Selly Oak, Birmingham, runs short and long courses on a wide variety of themes. 'Our course programme is designed to help you deepen your understanding of Quakerism, find support for your own personal and spiritual journey, and explore how faith and action work together in the world.' Marion McNaughton is a tutor in Practical Theology. It turned out that she not only had Quaker links with Marigold but that she had been brought up a Catholic and her mother had been a colleague of Pamela's at the Holy Child School in Edgbaston in the 1960s. Marion has much experience of organizing women's events and is an inspiring facilitator. At a women's weekend Marigold attended, Marion led a session on the ancient Jewish practice of *midrash* – deducing stories to fill in gaps in the

Bible narrative – and she gave us permission to print her story of Abraham and Isaac seen through Sarah's eyes (see below).

Practical theology?

'What do I do here? I encourage people to live their faith, put their faith into practice in the world, seeing what it means to them individually and to them in their community. This term we're looking at Quaker testimonies to peace, equality, justice, truth and integrity and really asking what it means to witness to your faith in the world. Very exciting.' That class is for both men and women but Marion told us that Woodbrooke regularly puts on short courses specifically for women.

Women building a multifaith Britain

The previous Saturday had been their annual Inter-faith Women's Day to which 60 women came – Jewish, Christian, Quaker, Muslim, Hindu and Buddhist. 'A little planning group meets regularly through the year. I think we meet more than we strictly need to because we like each other's company so much, so we eat food together, tell each other about our lives and plan the next conference. This one was called Women Building a Multifaith Britain. In the morning we have a speaker and discussion groups, so we're using our heads. After lunch we do lots of nurturing things: yoga, breathing, massage, painting. We end with a celebration – very moving. Lots and lots of tears, that's where I caught my cold – lots of hugging and kissing, sharing germs and hope! I think something like this shows us a way of living and sharing together, loving and trusting each other, learning from each other. Women of many generations in one room, and a lot of young women with children. The theme of the day was the city and the culture and the country that we want to build together. We were saying, "We're women of faith, of many faiths, and we think that's important. We want to help create a society where all faiths can flourish and affect things." We bring barriers in with us but they don't stay up long. When you love someone from another faith you can't put up a barrier against them.'

Work for encouragement and empowerment

Marion has been a teacher and an activist all her adult life. 'My gift is to be a teacher', she told us, 'to work for the encouragement and empowerment of people, to help people believe they can make a difference in the world. But I have to be out doing things as well.' Marion taught peace studies and women's studies at the University of Bradford and then spent four years in Philadelphia living (with her children) in a non-violent social change community (Philadelphia Life Center/Movement for a New Society). She learned the skills of non-violent social change and the training skills for passing them on, becoming training co-ordinator for a large organization called Women Organized Against Rape. In 1982 she returned to Britain because of cruise missiles, to share her skills with anti-nuclear groups.

Women religious challenging the status quo

Marion not only organizes radical women's activities, she nourishes her own spirit at other gatherings. 'I was on retreat with ten nuns and a progressive Jewish woman. The leader was a quite radical and forward-looking priest, but I noticed that the only people who challenged him were myself and the Jewish woman. At the end of the week one of the Sisters said to me, "At the beginning of the week, Marion, I thought what a pity you left the Church. But now I don't, now I think it's important that somebody leaves the Church if they have something to say, because they will listen to you but they won't listen to a Sister like me."

'On the Friday evening the Jewish woman said a Sabbath blessing over the bread and wine to share them and we sat and talked for the rest of the evening just as women. The Sisters were telling us the most exciting things they did – no more Mother Superiors or hierarchy, wonderful decision-making structures and egalitarian ways of operating – but only within their community, it hasn't touched the main structures of the Church. I asked an ordained Catholic friend about it later and he said, "Oh, the women are streets ahead of the men in the Catholic Church. The men are much too scared." But they still control everything.'

Two adjacent study groups

Marion had once been to a Jewish–Christian Bible study on Sarah. A woman rabbi took one group and a male rabbi the other, each with a Christian partner. Marion was disappointed to be put in the male rabbi's group but decided to give him a chance. 'The rabbi obviously wanted to make sure at the beginning that he wouldn't have any problem with feminists, so he said, "Before we begin I'd like to make it absolutely clear that although it's true that the Bible was written by men and all the commentaries were written by men, that doesn't mean that women are not fully present in all the Bible stories. Those men lived in a world where women were present and therefore everything that women thought or said is contained in the Bible."' In the stunned silence Marion said, 'I'm sorry, but I think that is complete rubbish' and made a little speech about women being consistently overlooked. But a terribly dreary Bible study ensued and at the coffee break Marion managed to transfer to the woman rabbi's group. 'She was doing wonderful things in her group and said, "Oh but there are Jewish women's prayers that we're only just discovering. There's a whole culture of Jewish women writing and doing their own thing." Two worlds, two adjacent study groups!'

'I believe things can happen'

An exciting part of Marion's voluntary work now is to be Chair of the Joseph Rowntree Charitable Trust's Racial Justice Committee which funds local and national groups working to address the causes of racial injustice.

'I've lost track of the number of times I've been told I'm naïve, because I believe in things, I believe things can happen. It seems quite clear to me that it is perfectly within our capability as human beings to create a beautiful, just society where everyone is fed. We have everything we need to do it – we're just not doing it. So because I know we can do it, I have to keep saying we can do it, expecting we can do it, reminding other people. Then they'll tell you you're being idealistic or naïve. You just pay no attention.'

Marion's midrash – Genesis 22

And with heavy heart Abraham went to his wife Sarah and said, 'God has told me to take our son Isaac, whom we love, and sacrifice him as a burnt offering.'

And Sarah said, 'A shrewd move. This God is no fool. This is Her way of testing you. What did you say to Her?'

And Abraham replied, 'I said nothing. I want God to know I will obey Him without question. I will do as He commands.'

And Sarah threw up her hands in despair and said, 'Abraham you are a bone-headed fool. What kind of a God do you think you are dealing with? What kind of a God would want you to kill your own son to prove how religious you are? Don't be so stupid! She's trying to teach you something: that you must challenge even the highest authority on questions of right and wrong. Argue with Her, wrestle with Her!'

But Sarah's words smacked to Abraham of blasphemy, and he went into the mountains with his son Isaac.

And Sarah said to God, 'Sister, you are playing with fire. He is too stupid to understand what you are up to. He won't listen to me and he won't challenge you; if you don't stop him, he will kill our precious son. Is that what you want?'

And God said, 'Sarah, they have a long journey to the mountains; I'm hoping one of them will see sense.'

And Sarah said, 'Like father, like son. You'll have to send an angel.'

And it came to pass as Sarah foretold, and the angel of the Lord spoke to Abraham the first time and told him not to kill his son. And Abraham sacrificed a ram as a burnt offering. And the angel of the Lord spoke to Abraham a second time and told him his off-spring would be as numerous as stars in the heavens and would possess the gates of their enemies.

And the angel of the Lord spoke to Abraham a third time and said, 'Because you were ready to kill your own son in the name of your God you will be known as a great patriarch and millions will follow your example. And they will believe that He is indeed a jeal-ous and a demanding God, and they will willingly sacrifice their sons in His name and to His glory. And there will be bloodshed and slaughter in all the corners of the earth.'

And Abraham returned to his wife Sarah and said, 'God is well pleased with me for I am to be a mighty patriarch.'

And Sarah said nothing. But she took the garments of Abraham and Isaac that were stained with the blood of the ram, and she carried them to the river to be washed. And the river ran red with the blood of generations to come, and Sarah wept bitterly.

And God came to Sarah at the water's edge and said, 'My sister Sarah, do not weep. You were right, it will take time. Meanwhile hold firm to what you know of me and speak it boldly. I am as you know me to be. Many generations will pass and a new understanding will come to the children of Abraham, but before then I shall be misheard and misrepresented except by a few. You must keep my truth alive.'

And Sarah dried her eyes and said, 'As if I didn't have enough to do.'

~~ 10 ~~

Household Names

We first went to the headquarters in Oxford of the County Federation of WIs to get a general picture from the County Chairman, Valerie Cantrell, and the County Secretary, Judith White, and were impressed by the range and quality of WI activities. 'Making a World of Difference' is their motto. As Valerie told us, 'The WI offers opportunities for all women to enjoy friendship, to learn, to widen their horizons and together to influence local, national and international affairs. That's our reason for being.' The WI is also non-sectarian and non-party-political (as events in June 2000 clearly showed!).

Although cooking and crafts are still important interests, WI members are involved in almost everything you can think of. We were astonished to read the list of mandates which have been adopted every year since 1918, some of them initiating national campaigns like Keep Britain Tidy. Judith told us that WI mandates sometimes come very early on in the public discussion of an issue. 'We've had a mandate about Aids for five or six years at least.' The four mandates for 1999 were on women's human rights; support for the failing agricultural industry; a five-year moratorium on GM crops; and ovarian cancer. Back in 1966 a mandate urged 'the government to investigate the present state of separated mothers and the difficulties and hardship they often have in obtaining maintenance money for themselves and their children'. Valerie told us, 'Once something has become a mandate it is incumbent on all WI members to do what they can to work towards it, whether as an individual, as a WI or as a county. A group of people all working towards the same thing is pretty powerful.'

Local WI monthly meetings usually include a speaker and Judith described the County's quality control system. 'For the last ten years we've had Speakers' Selection Days when half a dozen prospective speakers come and give their talk, or a sample of it, to WI members, who write down whether or not they think they ought to be in our Year Book. We now have a Year Book with a couple of hundred speakers. WIs also write in every year and tell us what speakers they've had and what they think of them.'

Valerie and Judith strongly approved of the famous Rylstone nude calendar which has raised huge sums for leukaemia research. 'It helped to dispel the feeling that WI is only jam,' said Judith, and Valerie added, 'People think WI members take themselves seriously, and we do when we're campaigning, but we can also laugh at ourselves!'

A local WI – Warborough and Shillingford (Oxfordshire)

Later, Marigold met with Liz Eaton and Mais Appleton in Warborough. Their WI has about 45 members and a committee of eight or nine. Liz described a typical monthly meeting: 'We start at 7.30 with what we grandly call 'the business', going through the Federation Newsletter, matters arising from previous meetings ... Then we have coffee or tea and then we have the speaker.' But both she and Mais give talks at other WIs and find that every single one is different – there is no set pattern.

In between meetings members are involved in countless activities like a voluntary car run to the surgery in Berinsfield, ferrying patients and collecting medicines five days a week. 'The WI is just women, you know,' stressed Liz, 'it's no big deal. It's just women who've found an umbrella to work under. They do a hundred other things. It's not that they're totally WI people.'

'If all the women who are involved in voluntary things said, "That's it, we'll do no more,' this country would just cease to function!" said Mais.

Associated Country Women of the World

All WI members are automatically members of Associated Country Women of the World. Mais is Oxfordshire's ACWW representative. Twice a year the County's International Sub-Committee organizes extremely popular days devoted to learning about a particular country, with two morning and two afternoon speakers. 'For the India day we actually had someone who brought all her Indian wardrobe since the day she was married, including her marriage clothes and her daughter's and we had a fashion show and wore them all. If they tell you that in India fashions don't change, don't believe it! It's as trendy as everything else!' Through ACWW members raise a lot of money for projects in developing countries. Oxfordshire recently funded a bore hole to provide clean water for a primary school in Swaziland and are already looking for another project. When Mais goes round fundraising she always tells members, 'These women are where we were in 1915, when the first WIs were formed – desperate to get together and do something to make a difference for their families and their communities – we owe it to them to give them a chance.'

WI – a valuable space

Liz reminded us that in the WI's early years many men saw it as a big threat: 'The women got married, they had their children, they stayed in the house and this was suddenly a way that they could get together and talk and the men didn't like it at all.' A friend of Mais' remembers her mother having to lie about going to WI – she said she was going to visit her sister but didn't say that her sister was going to WI!

The need for women to get together and do something for themselves is still strong. Liz said, 'It's a bit of our own time. I'm not an anti-man person at all, but it is nice that there is somewhere a woman can go where there are not going to be men because, bless them, they do try and take over! So I think WI is a very valuable space where women can talk about things and have a good giggle. You don't giggle the same with men, do you?'

People blossom in the WI

One gets the feeling that anything at all is possible within the WI. That's what Mais said about the WI's Denman College which will put on courses on whatever there is a demand for. 'If you've got enough get up and go you can get up and do anything.' Liz was Denman's representative for five years, going round telling WIs how wonderful it is. 'I've seen so many people absolutely blossom. It opens up so much, offers so much. Public speaking courses, for instance. When I came here there's no way I would have stood up to speak – and then you find yourself standing up in the town hall in front of 700 people! The first time I thought, "Shall I hurl myself down the stairs and see if I can break my arm? Perhaps they'd let me off if I had a broken arm."'

Liz's election as County Chairman was announced at Oxfordshire WI's AGM in March 2000, to which they kindly invited us. We had never before been in a gathering of 700 women, getting through a crowded agenda with calm efficiency in an atmosphere of joviality and enjoyment under Valerie Cantrell's serene and smiling guidance. (Liz herself was not there because she was in Jordan doing a very successful women-for-women sponsored bike ride in aid of the Queen Charlotte Hospital Appeal on behalf of women and babies. She told us later that it had been the experience of a lifetime, but a real test. They had cycled for five days and ended by getting up at 2 am to climb Mount Sinai (on foot) to watch the sun rise.)

As Liz said at our meeting, 'You can't take a single picture and say, "This is the WI." It's just made up of women, so different, so individual, such a variety of backgrounds. People don't want to believe it, but that's what it's about. We'll get there one day.' We feel sure they will, and hope they'll take us with them.

YWCA NATIONAL HEADQUARTERS IN OXFORD

The YWCA was founded in London in 1855 by two women, Lady Jane Kinnaird and Miss Emma Robarts. The first set up hostels specifically to provide accommodation for Florence Nightingale's nurses on their way to and from the Crimea. The second established Bible study groups to provide friendship and support to young women coming to London in service. We've all heard of the YWCA but do we know what it actually does now? It was extremely illuminating to speak with Dorrie Gasser, Assistant to the Chief Executive.

Creative tension and shifting emphases

She began by telling us about the creative tension the organization was experiencing between its Christian foundations and its open membership policy. 'Equal Opportunities legislation has impacted on us a lot. No longer, for instance, can we specify that staff should be Christian or that the young girls who come to us should be Christian (not that we ever did, but there was more of an emphasis on young white girls at one time).' The open membership policy led naturally, but not painlessly, to the decision to take Bibles out of hostel rooms. 'It was not an easy decision; we took it in good faith because on the one hand only a small minority of the young women in our hostels are Christians, and on the other we provide young girls with homes, we don't run hotels, so they have a right to decide what goes into their home. There was a storm of protest in the Christian press, but most people understood once we explained our point of view.' Dorrie believes that the value-base they now ask staff to subscribe to ensures that the organization still operates on Christian principles.

A further seismic change was related to the type of young woman the organization reached out to. 'Traditionally we used to house young women, either working or studying in large cities, who needed a safe, affordable place to stay. But over the last ten years the focus has shifted, and because our resources are limited, a decision was taken that we should focus them on young women in really desperate need.' Dorrie gave as an example of this shift a project in the East End of London: 'the Maze Project, which works with extremely young prostitutes – 13, 14, 15-year-olds; these girls are drug addicts and they have turned to prostitution as the only way they can feed their drug habit.'

A project in Truro runs a young women's centre which offers accommodation and help to young women with small children and women who are pregnant. It is run by a young woman who, said Dorrie, 'is not at all what you would think of as a typical member of the YWCA. She's young, she's fairly aggressive, she's up-front and she does the most amazingly valuable work for her young women. She subscribes to the YWCA's value-base, but she's not a Christian.'

The organization was, at the time of our meeting with Dorrie, going through another huge transition. 'Last December [1998] the Board of Governors decided that the YWCA should pull out of housing altogether. We will concentrate our resources on extending the range of welfare services that we already provide – anything from assertiveness courses to English classes for young Asian women, classes on health and so on, all basically to increase their self-esteem and their confidence and allow them to stand on their own feet.' Dorrie mentioned the women's centre in Loughborough which provides a whole range of services for women in the local community, many of whom are Asian. The Blue Triangle Centre in Loughborough was therefore our next port of call.

THE BLUE TRIANGLE CENTRE, LOUGHBOROUGH

The entrance hall displays colourful posters listing the many services and activities available here for mothers, teenagers and children. We arrived in time to have a word with some of the mums and toddlers who had enjoyed their Wednesday morning get-together. Next door the playgroup children were sitting in a circle singing. Ten out of the 17 were Asian. A waiting mother told us, 'Yes, it's good. They get on great. There's no reason why they shouldn't. Everybody's got to live together. They shouldn't be brought up to be "them and us". I don't think they notice any difference. We also celebrate the festivals of the different religions, which is good. We went to the temple down the road and we're learning lots of things about other people's cultures and religions.'

Person-centred counselling

The project manager, Maureen Hughes, is an excellent example of a woman becoming empowered herself and going on to help others do the same. She had left school at 15 with no qualifications, worked in factories, married and only discovered adult education courses via a mother and toddler group. She ended up with a university degree in History and Politics, and a qualification in Youth and Community Work. Maureen told us that the Centre's many years of providing pregnancy testing and sexual health information had become a wider counselling project for young women. 'I see our work here', she told us, 'as empowering women to come to a state in their lives when they feel they can make informed choices for their own advancement or well-being. Many come from dysfunctional families, or have been in care, or in abusive relationships. It's mostly about listening and believing them – helping them to move on from their problems, more than offering any instant cure. It's about building confidence, gaining self-worth.'

A self-satisfying job

Maureen's two Indian colleagues, Raekha and Urmila, had also worked hard, against tremendous odds, to get where they were. Raekha, convent-educated and with a degree in psychology and a BEd, came to Britain in 1992 to get married. Her Indian qualifications were not recognized so she took jobs and courses at the same time to get computer and secretarial skills, 'Yes, I have worked hard', she says. 'Because I have three kids it has been really difficult for me, but I have reached where I wanted to reach. Everything I have done has been used here.' She spoke of the good relationship between the Asian community and the English people in Loughborough, and of the different lifestyles of Asian and English women. 'We have to work harder than English women, because our men don't do anything in the house. Then we live in a joint family system where we have to look after our in-laws. But that also means I always have someone who will look after the children.'

Urmila had come to this country with her husband in 1968, when the Asians were expelled from Kenya. She had had a very hard time, working in factories, which she hated, and experiencing racism, which came as a shock to her. She had little self-confidence but her husband encouraged her to try for office jobs, which she enjoyed. When she lost her job for no good reason her self-esteem slumped again but she then got a job under a government Community Programme for unemployed people, followed by a job at an Asian Community Centre. Finally the Blue Triangle spotted her immense potential as a community worker and paid for her to become fully trained. Urmila, who speaks fluent Hindi, Punjabi and Gujarati, is now doing a counselling course and is already helping lots of women, 'Doing groups for them, counselling young women, encouraging unemployed women to do training, putting on training sessions and health days. This post is so varied, I'm really enjoying it. I've been here 13 years. It's very rewarding to see the difference you can help to make in women's lives. I can help, because I know what it feels like.'

~ 11 ~

The Wider World

Bridget Walker is joint Deputy Director of Responding to Conflict, an independent organization currently based at Woodbrooke Quaker Study Centre in Birmingham. RTC describes itself as 'an international, not-for-profit agency which provides practical capacity-building programmes to support people working for peace, rights and sustainable development in conflict-affected areas of the world'. Her previous experience in a fascinating variety of work has given her strong views on the position of women. When we asked her how she came to be where she is now, she put her hands together, thought a moment and started with her grandparents.

Education as a path to opportunity

'My grandmother was a servant in the house of a well-to-do family and my grandfather was the gamekeeper on the estate. My grandmother was determined that my mother should not be a servant so she saved and saved and when my mother got to be 14 she sent her to a secretarial college. So there was a strong sense in the female line of women being able to develop their potential, not just as wives and mothers but also for themselves. My mother married and had two daughters. Both my parents regretted having had no education beyond the age of 16. My father had got a scholarship to a secondary grammar school but the family couldn't afford to keep him on after the age of 16. So he supported my mother in the tradition of wanting a bit more for her daughters than she had had.'

In the 60s, as a result of Labour's educational policies, there were opportunities for young people from working-class families to

150

access higher education in a way that had not been possible previously, by providing grants for parents whose means were limited. 'So both my sister and I were able to stay on at school and go to university.' These educational opportunities were particularly important for girls, Bridget felt, since many people still thought that investing money in their education was not worth it. 'The availability of grants (not loans) helped challenge that. It also meant that young women were not lumbered with loan repayments later – at a time when they might want to begin families.

Finding women role models

'I was at college in the 60s, a time of all sorts of upheavals. I don't think I was aware of the women's liberation movement at that time, but I was deeply aware of the inequitable way I was treated in a mixed university college, after having been in a single sex school. After university I wanted to step outside my own culture so I went to Cameroon in West Africa as a volunteer with International Voluntary Service. That changed the way I looked at the world and also, interestingly, gave me some women role models I didn't see in my own society. There were a lot of women who were traders, who managed money, who ran a whole range of the business enterprise that was still a very male domain. At the same time there was a lot of abuse of women. I worked in a teacher training college where there were 400 male students and 40 female students, and I was one of only two women teachers. I had a very particular relationship with some of those women and got to know some of the pressures they were under. So that was the start of thinking about gender, and thinking about the world beyond our doorstep.

Women's role in development

'After I got home I worked for Christian Aid for seven years first as office manager and then as project officer for West Africa which took me back to francophone Africa. In 1975 – International Women's Year! – Christian Aid supported Marilyn Carr, of Intermediate Technology, to go and look at what women were doing with their own technology. Her book showed women doing things women here don't usually do, like blacksmithing, building your house, building a road, and of course all the technology around making utensils. At Christian Aid there was beginning to be some realization that "development" was not actually benefiting women but was disadvantaging them. For example, modernization was preventing women from providing for their families as cash crops took over land where they had grown subsistence crops.

'I remember going to Burkina Faso – then Upper Volta – and looking for projects, as one did then. Being a European female I tended to get treated a bit like an honorary male and I was talking to a group of village men about building a health post. They described their problems and were particularly concerned about maternal and child health. They said they would provide the labour to build the centre. We got it all worked out and I asked if I could talk to the women. "Oh! They don't talk French, they would be shy." "The teacher can translate." "They won't come and if they come they won't speak." They did come and they spoke for hours! I heard about every miscarriage, every labour that had gone on for three days, all the children that had died, it was harrowing. It was clear the women were behind the project and I was just saying, "These are the plans and this is where it's going to be", when a voice said, "Sister, where are they going to get the water at that place?" Believe it or not, the men who had drawn up the plans had not given a thought to water because water was what women carried and we've got women somewhere to carry it. So of course we had to change the plans. That convinced me more than anything else that you've got to involve women in planning to be both effective and equitable.'

Community in Brixton

After Christian Aid Bridget felt it was about time she did something in her own country and took on the job of overseeing the second stage of converting St Matthew's Church, Brixton, into St Matthew's Meeting Place, which was managed as a community meeting place by a committee of the user groups, which included two church congregations, the Anglicans and the New Testament

Assembly, a black-led Pentecostal church, among a range of other groups. 'What had started as a way of sharing space that the Anglicans could no longer use effectively, became an experiment in joint management.' The crypt had already been converted into a much needed large meeting-place where people of African and Caribbean descent could meet.

'I know it was the early 1980s, but there weren't many really big places where you could have a massive sound system and dance and bring in all the food and have a proper family rave-up without disturbing the neighbours.' (St Matthew's forms a large 'traffic island' near Brixton Town Hall.) The centre also had a play group, a truancy unit and a whole range of friendly societies, like the Star of Bethlehem Chapter. Bridget oversaw the building of an amphitheatre and a recreation hall so the building, as well as being a place of worship for two congregations (Bridget herself had worshipped there), became an important resource for many different community groups.

Back to Africa

The next move was to take time to reflect on experience by 'going back to school'. Bridget did a Master's course in Manchester on adult education and community development. Her dissertation, 'The Training and Education of Women in England – A Culture of Silence?' concluded that, though some change has occurred in England over the years, the balance of power is still much the same. After a few years' work as fundraiser for Quaker Peace and Service, Bridget went off to the Sudan with World University Service to co-ordinate education programmes for refugee women. 'That was a fascinating time. In our classes literacy was functional, based around experience and issues like health, so for instance the question of sexually transmitted disease, HIV, became something the women could talk about in their class. They wrote poems. I remember at graduation a woman getting up and saying how she'd been able to read a letter from her son whom she hadn't seen for years, and soon, soon, she'd be able to write one as well. We discovered how much sexual harassment went on, the atrocious way in which women refugees were expected to pay with their bodies for what are really entitlements. Often they had arrived with the man of their household and been registered in his name and then the man disappeared to get work. Because the women weren't on the list in their own name they weren't officially entitled to the food allowance and to get it they were forced to "pay" the authorities.'

Gender issues in times of crisis

Bridget had to come back from Sudan after one year. She joined Oxfam's gender unit and then, when that was merged into something else, the strategic planning team, 'or, as we called it, The Greater Gender Unit! I think the one thing I probably did that was new at Oxfam was try to work on issues to do with gender with colleagues who were responding to emergencies. Gender in development work was pretty well covered by then, but there was still the argument in emergencies, "You've got to respond rapidly so you can't think about things like that." Now, gender issues in times of crisis are on the agencies' agenda, though how far principles get translated into practice I don't know. Here at Responding to Conflict we have course participants who are encountering some of these ideas for the first time. It's a highly emotional time if you have come from a conflict situation and you're analysing that and talking about how to deal with it and on top of that having to sort out all the personal elements.'

We thanked Bridget for describing her extraordinary life. 'Well,' she said, 'if I lay it out like that, I think perhaps I did do something! I've been very lucky.'

ENGAGING WITH INTERNATIONAL ORGANIZATIONS

We started this book with one woman bringing different values into her immediate environment. We end with two women trying to bring different values into the international economic environment. Our friends Sophia Tickell and Wendy Tyndale, like us, had long worked on Latin America, and we met with them over dinner to hear about their current activities. Sophia first told us about her job at Oxfam:

'My job is partly to do with lobbying very large oil companies about the impact they have on the lives of the people directly affected by their operations. Oil exploitation often generates violent conflict as people fight to control the money it produces. Poor people's civil and political rights are affected, and their social and economic rights are neglected. Oil money ought to be providing schools and houses and health care, but more often than not it does not reach the poor – we try to find out why. In particular we were asked by Oxfam's Colombia office to look at British investment in the context of the conflict in Colombia so we've been studying the impact of British Petroleum's very large presence in the Casanare region. We have now made a series of recommendations to the company and we're waiting to see their response. They've been talking with us because they've been feeling the sting of very adverse publicity and were wondering what to do about it. To begin with they were mostly concerned about PR without a great deal of commitment to actually change things.

A meeting of different worlds

'The whole process,' Sophia told us, 'has been a meeting of people from completely different worlds learning how to speak to each other. To begin with, there was even a question of what we would wear, and what they would wear. I think they expected us to be eating lentils, and we thought their horns would be easily visible! We *had* to come to believe that it was possible to have some kind of common goal.' Sophia felt that a lot of the BP people they talked with wished it were possible for things to be better but she wondered how much power they had in the company. 'They tend to be people who are having this dialogue because they have active consciences, they want to act with integrity and they don't want their work to have such a negative impact. We have now got from the company the policy commitment to defend human rights that we were asking for, but until the people who manage the company's assets are told that it's all right to put money into these "soft issues" as they call them, I can't see any big change taking place. They always say, "There are other companies, and if we make ourselves very expensive, we'll be undercut."'

Keeping well-informed

For the Oxfam team to have credibility when talking with the giant company they need to have a clear sense of what is happening on the ground in Colombia. 'We need to have regular and reliable information from the region. That's been in some ways the most difficult bit, because it's very dangerous and people are being killed there. For people there to monitor the situation can be seen as subversive. But we are working with a network which we hope can provide a sustained flow of information.'

In a man's world

Women do not seem to have positions of any authority in the company's world so the men Sophia talked with did not know what to expect. 'One of the reasons we got as far as we did was because we don't even appear on their radar screen! I may be wrong in this but I did have a sense that we were not taken very seriously to begin with: there were a couple of very clear incidents where people were shocked by what we were saying. They had expected some little fillies to come into the room with some silly little observations but nothing particularly serious to put on the table.'

A clash of value systems

However, Sophia felt that they were bringing a different dimension into the discussion more because they came from a nongovernmental organization than because they were women. 'We were representing a very different value system. They found it difficult to understand how the value system Oxfam works to could be applied to them. *We* found it difficult to understand that you might have a value system but, because the world is a harsh place, leave it outside while you were doing your business. As NGOs we don't have the same compulsion to make money all the time. We in the NGOs are supported because of people's shared desire for the values to prevail. Where I do find the gender side relevant is when, as women, we are seen to uphold moral values. It is irritating when people say, 'You are our conscience!' as if they didn't have consciences themselves. Somehow I, as a woman, am to be the guardian of their moral sense, whatever it is.'

The religions and the World Bank

Wendy, whom we had known as head of the Latin America section of Christian Aid, has been Co-ordinator of the World Faiths Development Dialogue since it began in 1998. The WFDD describes itself as

> a dialogue between nine of the world's major religions and the World Bank. The subject is poverty and criteria for development policy and practice. Baha'is, Buddhists, Christians, Hindus, Jains, Jews, Muslims, Sikhs and Taoists are all concerned about the unacceptable levels of poverty in our world, and about the ever-increasing gap between the rich and the poor. The World Bank shares this concern and, for the first time in its history, has opened its doors for a dialogue with the faiths.

This is an exciting initiative, but extremely difficult and delicate. Wendy agreed with Sophia: 'One of the biggest difficulties has been trying to communicate in a way that makes sense to both sides in the dialogue. The first meetings we had with people from the World Bank and North American economists left us with the impression that we had been talking past each other on two parallel roads that never met, and we had no idea how to make those conversations merge. It has happened because we stuck to our viewpoint. Had we tried to incorporate more economists or take over more of their ground, we wouldn't have been able to. We have very helpful economists working with us but we've been able to argue our standpoint using completely different arguments, which many people in the WB have found very valid.'

'The World Bank is not a monolith'

'That is one of the biggest things I've learnt. Inside this institution is, for example, a group which meets every Friday from 8 to 9 am to discuss ethical issues in the WB's work. Most of them come from religious backgrounds, but not all. Those people are delighted by this dialogue and very keen that we should open more windows and create more stir. Also in various meetings people have suddenly said, "For us, culture is the thing that the WB is missing. A lot of the mistakes of the Bank in Africa are due to the fact that we've been unaware that we are dealing with people whose vision of the world is completely different from ours, and for whom what is important are things we don't even think of." So we have a lot of potential allies there, and it's a case of knowing tactically and strategically how to do the work best.'

Maintaining a critical judgement

Sophia feels that for all their goodwill and integrity, it is very hard for allies within BP or the WB really to bring about change from within. Wendy believes that what happens to people in the WB could very readily happen to her. 'They go in thinking they are going to change the world, change the culture of the WB, and little by little are forced into making concessions so as not to live as complete schizophrenics. They become satisfied with far less than they had hoped for and say, "Well we've done something that wasn't actually negative so I am justified in earning this enormous salary and flying round the world first class." It's essential in this job to maintain a very critical judgement about one's own role. If you lose that you can get sucked in without even noticing it, until you have no idea what you are doing. I find the Hindu idea of detaching yourself from glory or disaster very helpful. You do your best and have a very clear goal, but your whole being isn't bound up in the result, because I think that's the first step to losing perspective and not being able to judge where to go next.'

Just one ant in a big heap

Wendy has been much strengthened in her work by discovering a network of solidarity wherever she goes. 'In India I was very moved to hear people saying the same things I heard in Latin America. A memorable occasion was with some very poor women in a rural village, who knew exactly what the WB was and said, "Our message is, could you tell the President of the World Bank that his money never reaches us." I felt that the world is globalized and the same things are being fought for in lots of different places. In Sri Lanka it was the same. That is very encouraging because it makes you feel that individual efforts are important, but only as part of the enormous ant heap.

Being a woman – advantage or disadvantage?

'Being an *old* woman is an advantage! Because of my grey hair people think I'm very old and that gives you some kind of authority, which has been very useful. People have said to me, "I'm amazed at an old lady like you travelling round the world." This was good because practically all the meetings I went to in India were just men. I found it daunting, as Sophia said, because you wonder what you should wear and whether you are doing all the wrong things, but I haven't found it an obstacle. I'd have liked other women to be there because women see the world in a different way, and you do feel there is a one-sided picture in the religions. I have never been so aware of the male domination inside the religious institutions as I am now. But I'm also extremely aware of the gap between the religious institutions and people of a spiritual life who belong to these traditions. Even looking at the Church of England, what that represents doesn't say anything about the life of its members or the spirituality they generate around them.

People must be at the centre

'The constant message from all NGOs, especially the faith-based ones, is that people must be at the centre of the development process. There's no point in applying economic theories without taking into account every dimension of human beings, including the spiritual. If you're going for cost-effectiveness and you think it's a waste of time for people to spend half the day praying on the mountain, because they're not earning money, you'll either alienate those people completely from the process you want to promote, or you'll undermine their roots until they're lost in a system they don't understand.

'I've often told the story of some Guatemalan women who were working in a project. The economist arrived one morning to take their hens to market, because the earlier you got to market the better price you got. The women were scandalized because they hadn't blessed each of the hens before they left. So they had the blessing ceremony: "Carlota, we bless you on your way to market" and so on. When they finished they'd missed the market altogether for that week, but if they had not had that process they would have left the project. For them, the blessing of the hens was much more important than earning a better price.

'So there are two, in fact many, completely different systems operating. The faith-based organizations need to learn that message too because all religions speak about being inclusive and welcoming the stranger but are often extremely bad at doing it! This dialogue could provoke a lot of discussion among the religions if people are open enough. Although there are some fundamental differences, there are an enormous number of things in common: "Do to your neighbour as you would be done by", for instance.'

Are we on the right track?

Wendy and Sophia had an interesting discussion about the value of the path of engagement with large institutions which they are both following. Sophia knows many people who say that it is completely misguided ('All you're doing is allowing yourself to be hoodwinked effectively') but she is convinced that the best way to persuade people is by making a good case. 'Bombarding offices will only make them feel they're under siege and refuse to consider alternatives'. Wendy fears that trying to persuade people through words is very difficult and that it is important to bring people into contact with the reality of other people's lives. Sophia described the self-sufficient fenced-off compounds within which BP employees exist: 'What I've most wanted to do is to disguise the BP people as normal NGO people and let them hear what other people are saying about the impact they are having – I'm sure their views would change.'

That may be difficult to imagine in BP, but in the WB something similar is now happening. 'James D. Wolfensohn, the present President, has decided that every senior member of staff has to live at least a fortnight in a shanty town, or peasant community. Apparently it's having an enormous effect on them. In Ethiopia the local office of the WB had had no contact with the religions there and were very sceptical in the beginning, but it's opening up new vistas and giving them access to poor communities which they would never have had before. Which doesn't mean to say that we want the religions to be channels into poor communities for the WB's policies. We have to be as wise as serpents, that's the problem.

'If you say that an effort towards some engagement with enormously powerful bodies is not the way forward,' Wendy believes, 'it's hard to see any role except as a protest movement. It's easy to denounce and we've all done it. I've done a tremendous amount of militant campaigning in my life. Maybe it's a historical change around us, but I feel the time has come when we must somehow be more inclusive in how we try to achieve change, or all you do is set up constant barriers. And since we are on the far side of those barriers, we'll always lose.'

Sophia and Wendy exemplify the principle guiding the women whose stories we have heard: rather than following a grand plan, a pre-designed strategy, their simple rule is to put people first, and shape the plan accordingly. Facing the world of global economic affairs with *its* grand plan, Sophia and Wendy and their colleagues calmly advance a different vision, a different set of values. They seek to make the real people who run big businesses and institutions (which for them are 'the real world') aware of the effects of their plans and strategies on other real people in other utterly different 'real worlds'.

Paradoxically, 'making a difference', for the women in this book, means breaking down differences, recognizing connectedness, bringing different realities into contact, working towards a single 'real world' in which we can all feel at home.

Epilogue

Oh God
Where hearts are fearful and confined:
  Grant freedom and daring.
Where anxiety is infectious and widening:
  Grant peace and reassurance.
Where impossibilities close every door and window:
  Grant imagination and resistance.
Where distrust shapes every understanding:
  Grant healing and transformation.
Where spirits are daunted and dimmed:
  Grant soaring wings and strengthened dreams.

Addresses

ANAWIM,
166 Mary Street,
Balsall Heath,
Birmingham B12 9RJ
Tel.: 0121 440 5296

Ark–T, Tuesday Art Group,
John Bunyan Baptist Church/
The Ark–T Centre,
Crowell Rd, Cowley,
Oxford OX4 3LN
Tel.: 01865 773499

The Cathedral Centre,
Salford Cathedral,
250 Chapel Street,
Salford M3 5LL
Tel.: 0161 839 4191

Catholic Women's Network,
National Contact: Veronica Seddon,
42 Priory Road, Hampton,
Middlesex TW12 2PJ
Tel./fax: 020 8979 5902

Cedarwood Trust,
43 Avon Avenue, Meadow Well,
North Shields,
Tyne and Wear NE29 7QT
Tel.: 0191 259 0245

The Furnival,
199 Verdon Street,
Sheffield S3 9QQ
Tel.: 0114 272 7497; fax: 0114 278 4769

Heartstone,
'Mayfield', High Street,
Dingwall, Ross-shire IV15 9ST,
Scotland
Tel.: 01349 865400; fax: 01349 866066

Lighthouse Project,
3/4 Block 11, Andrew Road,
Halesowen, West Midlands B63 4TT
Tel.: 01384 358383/4; fax: 01384 358383
Email: lighthouse@halesowen35.freeserve.co.uk

'My Kids & Me', Joanne Wilkins,
c/o 7 Waltham Place, Blakelaw,
Newcastle-upon-Tyne NE5 3RR
Tel.: 0191 242 4383

Oxfam,
274 Banbury Road,
Oxford OX2 7DZ
Tel.: 01865 311311; fax: 01865 312600

Oxfordshire Women's Aid,
PO Box 255,
Oxford OX1 1AS
Tel.: 01865 791416

Oxford Women's Training Scheme,
The Northway Centre,
Maltfield Road,
Oxford OX3 9RF
Tel.: 01865 741317; fax: 01865 742199
Email: owts@globalnet.co.uk

RAP Community Action,
74–77 Magdalen Road,
Oxford OX4 1RE
Tel.: 01865 242950
Email: rapaction@hotmail.com

Street Cred,
Jennifer Kavanagh,
The Parlour, 45–47 Blythe Street,
London E2 6LN
Tel./fax: 020 7729 9267

UNLOCK,
Unlock House,
336A City Road,
Sheffield S2 1GA
Tel.: 0114 276 2038; fax: 0114 276 2035

Urban Theology Unit,
210 Abbeyfield Road,
Sheffield S4 7AZ

Women's Institutes, National Federation of,
104 New Kings Road,
London SW6 4LY
Tel.: 020 7371 9300; fax: 020 7736 3652

Women's Institutes, Oxfordshire Federation of,
11 Middle Way, Summertown,
Oxford OX2 7LH
Tel.: 01865 556608; fax: 01865 511754

Woodbrooke Quaker Study Centre,
1046 Bristol Road, Selly Oak,
Birmingham B29 6LJ
Tel.: 0121 472 5171; fax: 0121 472 5173
Email: enquiries@woodbrooke.org.uk
Web: www.woodbrooke.org.uk/woodbrooke

World Faiths Development Dialogue (WFDD),
33–37 Stockmore Street,
Oxford OX4 1JT
Tel./fax: 01865 790011
Email: wfdd@btinternet.com

YWCA Blue Triangle Centre,
Great Central Road,
Loughborough LE11 1RW
Tel.: 01509 212517/212592
Email: rum@wcalbro.freeserve.co.uk

YWCA National Headquarters,
Clarendon House, 52 Cornmarket Street,
Oxford OX1 3EJ
Tel.: 01865 304200; fax: 01865 204805